THOSE PEARLY ISLES

The Story of the Enchanting Elizabeth Islands

by

Harold C. Wilson

A Publication of the

Gosnold Society of Cape Cod, Inc.

North Falmouth, Mass., U.S.A.

Cover photograph courtesy of Benjamin S. Harrison

Revised Third Edition June 1976

Library of Congress Card Number 74-80479

International Standard Book

Number 0-9600760-2-6

Printed in the United States of America
by Kendall Printing, Inc.
Falmouth, Massachusetts

TABLE OF CONTENTS

LIST OF PLATES

(Pages 55 - 71)

My contribution to
America's 200th Birthday

ACKNOWLEDGEMENTS

Many people, librarians, scholars, and friends, have contributed encouragement, help, and advice in the preparation of this book. For their generosity, I owe them my total gratitude.

However the following people deserve special mention because without their sincere assistance, this book would not have been possible: My mother, Mary, who from the very beginning, encouraged me to continue my study of the Elizabeth Islands; my wife, Janet, who somehow managed to tolerate my nasty temperament when things got rough. The students of the New Bedford, Massachusetts, Public Schools who provided needed inspiration; the members of *Naushon Trust,* present owners of many of the Elizabeth Islands, especially Mr. David C. Forbes of Boston, who gave me the opportunity to explore the interesting landscape of Naushon Island; Mrs. Alice Barton Gormley of Brookline, Massachusetts, who proofread the manuscript; Mr. E. Gale Huntington of Vineyard Haven on Martha's Vineyard for his priceless advice on preparing the manuscript for publication; and finally, the Dukes County Historical Society at Edgartown, especially Miss Dorothy Scoville, Mrs. Margaret Chatterton, and Mrs. D. Osborn Bettencourt, for their kind assistance and cooperation at the Society's library where I spent many hours studying materials for the book.

AUTHOR'S NOTE

Only a short distance from contaminated land, air, and water, the Elizabeth Islands are a shining example of natural preservation. They symbolize a total healthy environment. They are unique because their unspoiled forests and meadows have been sensibly maintained over the centuries. Extending westward out to sea from Woods Hole, Massachusetts, they resemble a string of pearls partially because the landscape of the five larger Elizabeths contain millions of sparkling mineral stones. Their shoreline winds here and there forming many coves and inlets which are adorned with silvery beaches. Their wooded hollows and green moors are embellished with Sassafras, Holly, Dogwood, both Red and White Cedar, Witch Hazel, Velvety Oak, Princess Pine, Honeysuckle, and Bayberry. Animals of land, air, and sea include Red-Necked Turkeys, White Swans, and Blue Crabs. In short they are not only beautiful but infinitely precious in our age.

This book is a *love story,* my love story with the Elizabeth Islands. It is my hope that after reading the book, the reader will share my conviction that Those Pearly Isles must not be changed. There is the possible danger of their becoming *abused,* when they should be *used,* effectively, to demonstrate the true esthetic value of our environment.

The book will attempt to describe the Elizabeth Islands, Naushon, Pasque, Nashawena, Penikese, and Cuttyhunk, to detail my own personal discoveries of these islands, and to give the stories of others who loved the islands as I do. I am admittedly far from the first, and one of the least distinguished lovers of the islands. But my story, like theirs, is characterized by a close association between man and nature. I hope that these stories might help in the perpetual preservation of the Elizabeth Islands.

Harold C. Wilson
North Falmouth, Massachusetts
May 28, 1973

Chapter One

GOSNOLD'S HOPE

We know that Gosnold was entranced
By beauties of this Greek-blue Bay,
And to our own time has advanced
The heart-felt tribute Cape men pay.

Langley Carleton Keyes
Cape Cod Passage, 1969

Buzzards Bay is a sparkling body of water. When the wind is low, and the sun is high, it reflects a dazzling light. In summer, even when the sun is down and the quarter moon is partially hidden by low clouds, the Bay's many coves and inlets sparkle with a luminous brilliance. The reason for the night brilliance is the presence of a microscopic creature called *Noctilina Scintillins* which has the ability to become phospherescent when the water is warm enough. I like to call these animals the "fireflies of the water."

In winter when a long freeze has prevailed, the bay turns to ice, quite solid in many places. On a sunny day, one cannot stare too long at this sight because of the awesome reflection of silver and white. Many times I have ventured to the shore and walked upon the almost plastic-like chunks of ice and snow that pile up on the beaches. One can, if he dares, walk onto the bay a considerable distance on this spongy crust. In such weather, the many rocks and boulders along the beaches are covered with frozen spindrift and appear like frosted potatoes.

Sometimes the Bay can become very gray and "dirty" especially in spring and early summer. The prevailing winds from the southwest are provided with a long enough fetch so that the surface of the water becomes upset with mean looking waves. This makes it uncomfortable for boatsmen.

The Bay, of course, provides the Elizabeth Islands with a north shore line. Vineyard Sound provides the south shore line.

1

However, I am interested in the Bay side and the Bay itself because I am not an authority on the Sound but have information to offer on Buzzards Bay.

The Elizabeth Islands are remnants of the last Ice Age some 10,000 years ago. The gigantic ice sheets plucked and pushed rocks, soil, and boulders south from New Hampshire and Maine like a bulldozer moving dirt and gravel. When the ice began to recede and melt, the sea commenced to rise. Geologists tell us that at one time, what is now the Elizabeth Islands was a single peninsula jutting from the mainland (See Plate I). Gradually the sea broke through the more vulnerable areas, and along with current and wave action, shaped the island group to what they look like today. The many rocks and boulders that tumbled from the banks of the islands over the past, now provide a "buffer zone" against the sea to limit any future extensive erosion. So it looks like the Elizabeth Islands' shore line won't change much for many years to come.

The Bay's waters cover the remains of some dead or partially dead Elizabeth Islands. Sow and Pigs Reef extending from the western side of Cuttyhunk now is under water. The sea has claimed most of what used to be a larger Weepecket Island. Only some broken rocky bones are visible today. At the eastern end of Naushon, several small isles have disappeared because of the swirling and surging motion of the sea. Today, only the skeletons of those former islets, isles and islands remain.

The Bay is used by man for fishing and shell-fishing, sailing and pleasure boating, plus other forms of recreational activities including bathing. Large tankers and freighters lumber along east or west, either heading towards or moving away from the Cape Cod Canal. The fish are rather plentiful. Besides the sport fish, namely, Blues and Striped Bass, one can drop a hook and sinker to the sandy bottom and catch Flounder, Fluke, or Scup. Apparently Whales were also plentiful in the Bay at one time. John Winthrop, former owner of Naushon in the early seventeenth century, mentioned that the Indians told him that a white Whale was kept in Westend Pond on his island, long before the English came to America. How it got there is a mystery. Once in a while, a hungry shark, prowling a short distance off shore, will chase summer folk away from the beaches. But this happens infrequently and only when the water is extremely warm.

2

Shellfish are less abundant. Since the beginning of this century, overfishing and chemical pollutants have taken their toll. It is often backbreaking work to catch the legal limit of Quahogs or Steamers. However, the Rock Oyster seems to be making a comeback, especially along the West Falmouth shore, and perhaps wise conservation will build up their numbers. The fickle Bay Scallop with its short lifespan of eighteen months, is usually available for shellfishermen between October and March, but one can never tell.

A very underrated shellfish, the blue/black Mussel, is found in abundance all along the shore. This underdog of the Bay's inlets and coves lives on rocks, pilings, and anything else it can grab on to. Steamed in a mixture of red wine vinegar, broth and green olives, Mussels have provided the author with many memorable moments in good eating. Soon, there could be an awakening of interest in them. If this happens, I hope we will learn from our mistakes with their cousins, the clams, and cull them with care.

Other interesting forms of sealife like Blowfish, Sea Robins, Fiddler Crabs, Hermit Crabs are also plentiful. Many of the marshes are simply overrun with life of both sea and land. The Horseshoe Crab, related to the spider, descendent of those that roamed the earth millions of years ago, slides through the mud and sand seeking out its favorite food, the clam. Even the Lobster roams the shadowy bottom of the bay at night. But few of them remain, and they are difficult to catch in numbers, which was not the case in days gone by.

In the sixteenth and early seventeenth centuries, Europeans thought there was a colossal Indian kingdom where Buzzards Bay and the Elizabeth Islands are today. They called it Norembega. Many courageous (and expensive) attempts were made to find it, but all were failures. A broad river with its opening near 40 degrees north latitude, they believed, would lead them to this domain and its vast riches. Gold and silver, along with many other valuable commodities, were to be had for the asking. It was thought that the river of Norembega might even take them to the Pacific Ocean—a Northwest Passage to the East Indies. The climate was supposed to be similar to southern Spain, where people could live in comfort while tending their vineyards.

In 1524, Giovani Da Verrazzano, an Italian working for France, sailed up the east coast of the present-day United States.

He discovered the Hudson River and then stayed a short time in Narragansett Bay. When sailing for home, he passed eastward of Cape Cod completely undershooting Buzzards Bay. No Norembega was found.

In 1583, Sir Humphrey Gilbert, an Englishman working for himself, set out on a voyage with five ships loaded with people and supplies. Besides making money, one of his aims was to colonize Norembega. However, Gilbert's fleet met with tragedy off Nova Scotia, and he, along with four of his ships, were lost in a severe gale. The expedition was a complete disaster.

It was not until 1602 that the first recorded white man entered and explored Buzzards Bay. This distinction goes to Captain Bartholomew Gosnold, another Englishman. At the moment he entered the Bay, his companions honored him by calling it Gosnold's Hope. The name had a double significance: Hope is an old English word meaning haven or bay; and since the explorers thought they were in the general vicinity of Norembega, they had high hopes of finding it. However, they soon were disappointed when they ran into a dead end at the head of the Bay where the towns of Marion and Wareham are now located. Captain Gosnold, after building a trading station and fort on the shore of the Bay, was soon persuaded by his associates to return to England. Reluctantly, he ordered his men to load the ship with sassafras, cedar logs, and other sundry commodities and sailed for home after only a short three week stay.

But Gosnold had the key to the door of English colonization and is credited with opening it. His reports of the voyage, published in England, described the country in glowing terms: a place where nature had outdone herself, creating a scene of beauty hardly natural. Soon many voyages followed Gosnold. In 1620, the Pilgrims found Plymouth, and eventually the land was taken away from the Indians who never really owned it, anyway. They just used it better than anyone else.

How the word Buzzards became attached to the word Bay to form Buzzards Bay is a mixed up story. The Indians called it, Poughkeeste (bay with coves). In the 1600's it was called Manomet or Monument Bay, presumably for a Manomet Indian tribe who lived at the head of the Bay. It is known that Governor Mayhew of the Massachusetts Bay Colony designated it Monument Bay in 1686. However, these names did not stick and in

4

the early to mid 1700's, it was called Fishhawk Bay for the osprey, a bird similar in looks to a buzzard. In fact, the early settlers called this bird "buzzardet" or little buzzard. Apparently the word buzzardet was simplified to Buzzards and used by map and chart makers for the name of the Bay. This happened in the late 1700's, and the name hasn't changed since. Another remote possibility is that a family of people named Buzzard lived on the shores of the bay in the 1700's. In fact, I have been told that the Bay was named in their honor.

If however the question of renaming the bay ever arises, we should seriously think of calling it either Pocasset Bay, the shortened version of Poughkeeste, in honor of the Indians or Gosnold's Bay in tribute to Captain Bartholomew Gosnold, the leading English colonial pioneer who discovered it. I suppose if the Bay was named for a man called Buzzard, and if he is found to be of creditable character, then the name probably shouldn't be changed. But if the name is found to be for the bird Buzzard, a bird which never existed here, then it should be altered to commemorate those that discovered the Bay, lived around it and loved it. All were impressed with its many inlets and coves which provide excellent harbors. The Bay, itself, is actually a great harbor with several smaller ones projecting from it, on all three sides.

However, the focus of this book is the sixteen mile stretch of broken land called the Elizabeth Islands between which are passages that allow the water of the Bay to gush through to Vineyard Sound. These little pearls with their green carpets of Tansy and Grass sprinkled with Pine and Sassafras, begin with the tiny isles of Uncatena and Nonamesset near Woods Hole in Massachusetts.

Chapter Two

AN INTIMATE LOOK AT DISCOVERY

Pearl of the southern sea,
Isle of beauty and mystery,
With your green carpet of tansy and grass,
Sprinkled with beech and sassafras,
Do you have at your western side,
Buried near the outgoing tide,
Something left in haste,
By purposed men of rare taste?

Harold C. Wilson
1971

Naushon is the largest of the Elizabeth Islands being eight miles in length and from three-quarters-of-a-mile to two miles in width. On its eastern side, near Woods Hole, Massachusetts, there are several baby isles, some loosely and some not so loosely, connected to the mother island. Nonamesset and Uncatena, the larger of these infants form a gateway into Hadley Harbor, Naushon's main port of call. Tarpoulin Cove, midway down the island's south side and Kettle Cove on the opposite northern side, are the largest of many such coves found on Naushon's coastline.

I love Naushon. Apparently many others also admired this island's natural beauty. Before the English came to America, the Indians would bring their families to the island for a summer vacation. When Gosnold and his men left Naushon they did so "with true sorrowful eyes." Oliver Wendal Holmes called it "the most splendid domain that anyone could look upon in these latitudes." Ralph Waldo Emerson dreamed within its shady retreats. General Sheridan, of Civil War fame took his last horseback ride there, shortly before his death. Henry David Thoreau, in his short visit to Naushon in 1856, was surprised by the island's "noble primitive wood."

From an airplane, flying east to west only five hundred feet in altitude, one can observe, at a glance, the island's gifts to man. All along the outside of the island, fifty to two hundred yards from the shore, one sees many plain fields of grass with herbs and shrubs, including Huckleberry, Strawberry and Mountain Cranberry. In the interior, one can see the many clusters of Beech trees with scattered Cedar, Oak, and Hickory. Here and there, are many exposed meadows, some of them very large. If one has a keen eye, he will see a deer or two dart into the woods, startled by the roar of the plane. On approaching the west end of the island, the pilot must be cautious of the many seagulls flying in the area. They breed on the rocks below, at Crescent Beach.

A few seconds later there appears a lake, some 45 acres in area, called Westend Pond. Many ducks and even a few swan may be dotting its surface. As the plane now roars over the west end of the island, one sees a definite contrast between the flowering bushes and the blossoming trees of Naushon and the barren looking, rocky terrain of Pasque Island, less than 1000 feet across the narrow channel called Robinson's Hole.

Now, let us get down to earth and take an intimate look at Naushon. The remainder of this chapter as well as chapter three will describe my experiences and observations on the island during a two-day excursion there on 25 and 26 October 1969. Incorporated into the description will be events of two previous trips which took place in August of the same year.

Around noontime on 25 October, Mr. David C. Forbes and a group of duck hunting friends deposited me on the western shore of Naushon at Robinson's Hole. Mr. Forbes, chairman of *Naushon Trust,* who owns the island, was interested in my theory that Captain Bartholomew Gosnold may have built his settlement on the bank of the Westend Pond rather than at Cuttyhunk which previous historians had claimed. He had already graciously allowed me to explore the area in question a few times in August. But these had been short trips, lasting only a few hours each. Therefore, upon my request, Mr. Forbes gave me the opportunity to spend a longer overnight stay on the island to allow me to investigate the place in more detail. He also gave me permission to use the then vacant farmhouse at Robinson's Hole as a home base and a place to spend the night. The house was conveniently less than a mile from Westend Pond. I was to fend for myself concern-

7

ing the long eight mile trip back to Hadley Harbor on the east end. The next day the ferry was scheduled to leave for the mainland at four o'clock in the afternoon. My knapsack contained food and supplies, sufficient for the two-day exploration.

Although the visibility was poor because of low clouds, I could see the cliffs of Gay Head on Martha's Vineyard, six miles distant across the Sound. The bleak dome of Pasque Island faced me across Robinson's Hole to the west. A brisk southwest wind was blowing, keeping the temperature at a somewhat comfortable 49 degrees. The summer had been a long one, and as a result many of the trees and bushes were reluctant to drop their foliage. In fact, many of the leaves still had much of their green color, although they were streaked with yellow. The rolling hills around me were covered with low bushes showing their red, green, and purple softness. I was alone.

After a short survey of the surrounding area, I entered the farmhouse and deposited my belongings, lingering long enough to eat a quick lunch of cold chop suey and horseradish. The food was washed down with a few ounces of a good Russian beverage.

From my supplies, appeared a pair of work gloves, one apple, a field compass, a topographic map, three short lead pencils and a notebook. I also collected binoculars, a hunting knife, a rope, and a quahog rake. The decision was to spend the better part of the afternoon at Westend Pond allowing plenty of time for the return trip to the house before sunset. With supplies firmly attached army style and still wearing my hip boots, the one mile walk to the pond began.

During the walk, a short cut through the bush seemed wise. This was a mistake. A few times, I found myself almost hopelessly entangled in crawling Bull Briar and thorny Rose Hip Bushes. As a result of this unnecessary excursion, I probably expended at least 20 percent of my total energy for the day.

Within an hour a small group of sand dunes located at the southern end of West Beach just 1,000 feet west of the Pond was reached. On the highest dune, I stood observing the general area. To the west and northwest was the beach itself, consisting of fairly fine sand, although somewhat granular in places. It curved rather sharply forming a shoreline for a cove, the water of which was only slightly shaken by the sharp wind from the southwest. To

8

the east, separated from me by a large patch of wet swampy land covered with blueberry and other bushes, was an old sheep grazing field. It couldn't be seen then, because of some larger trees blocking the view. But I knew it was there, from an earlier visit. A grove of young Black Oak, some 15 feet in height, stood a short distance to the right. In front and northerly was a large fresh water swamp with a puddle-like pond in its midst. Both the swamp and the puddle lie between the ocean to the west and some high ground, forming the bank of Westend Pond, to the east. Westend Pond, of course, was completely obscured from view because of the thick woods that surrounded it.

There were no rocks except for the boulders that boarded the north and south side of the cove. I later recalled that I did not find one old beer can lying on the beach anywhere. In fact, there was no evidence that people ever visited the place, except for the bridal path running over the dunes and disappearing along the outermost parts of the beach.

Anxious to arrive at the Pond, I started to walk along the edge of the swamp. My curiosity was alerted by some exposed logs and debris a few yards into the swamp. I decided to investigate and attempted to cross a small winding creek. However, about midway across the creek I began to sink, rapidly, into the quicksand like bottom. I was completely stuck up to the tops of my hip boots, and with any movement, the mud would only take a firmer grip. I felt helpless. Fortunately, the quahog rake saved the day. Using it as a lever and hook, I managed to fasten the business end to the opposite bank about six feet away. With a desperate but determined effort, I pulled myself out of the muck.

Without hesitation, I circled the swamp, walking north and then east towards the bank of the Pond. For a moment my attention was alerted, by two grazing sheep on some higher ground near the swamp. In making an attempt to approach, they immediately scampered off into the brush. There are a considerable number of sheep running wild all over the island. A stranger, visiting here and unaware of this, could get quite a shock especially when one of them suddenly appears from nowhere out of the underbrush.

I finally reached the Pond on its western side. This location is where I supposed Captain Bartholomew Gosnold and his men had built their settlement in 1602. The west bank of the Pond is actually a heavily wooded plot of ground about an acre and a half in area. Many old Beech, Oak, Maple, and other trees are found rotting on the ground. This oval shaped plot forms a cliff, facing the Pond. From north to south, the cliff gradually attains a height of 20 feet and then tapers off practically to sea level. Several rocks and boulders are found at the base of the cliff, sitting on a fine sandy bottom. The water depth here is about two to three feet.

A bridal path bisects the plot running north to south. The entire path is shaded by a heavy growth of trees on both sides. Many large rocks are found nearby, especially where the path reaches the highest point. A small fieldstone bridge spans a narrow ditch that cuts across this portion of the island from the Pond to the beach. It is located on the extreme north side of the plot. On the south end there is a natural sand deposit which forms a small beach and is used as a watering place by deer and other animals. With the Pond on its east side, and the swamp to its west, and the low features to the north and south, the plot resembles that of a small isolated islet.

My purpose was to investigate possible sites where the Gosnold explorers might have built a fort and house large enough to accommodate about twenty men.

I first waded along the base of the cliff in two or three feet of water. Occasionally, I drifted farther out from the cliff to sketch on my pad the tree line of the plot. A dip in the line would indicate a possible "clearing" where man had interfered with nature by cutting down trees. Going back and forth along the bank for several minutes, I eventually located the highest point of the cliff and decided, then, to explore the entire plot.

Thinking a rope was not necessary, I slowly and carefully began to climb the steep bank. It was, here, near the crest of the cliff that I suffered my second hazard of the afternoon. Attempting to use my quahog rake as a grappling hook, to grasp the top of the precipice, I lost my balance and fell backward, hurtling some fifteen feet into the water. For an instant, I was flat on my back and partially submerged in two feet of water. Pulling myself up quickly, I sat on a flat-topped rock nearby. No physical damage had been done and the hip boots saved me from being completely drenched.

10

After several minutes, a second attempt was made; and learning from the mistakes the first time, I successfully conquered the cliff. It was now time to investigate the rocky terrain of the plot. It was impossible to search along the edge of the cliff because of thick bushes and vines. Therefore, I walked a short distance west to the bridle path and followed it north to the lowest point of the islet and blasted, if that is the proper word, my way through fifteen feet of heavy underbrush to the bank of the Pond. Although it was late October, there were many grapevines with purple fruit. They tasted sweet and juicy. I rested for a while, sitting on a small rock, and looked out at the Pond. The most striking feature was its apparent crystal clear water. Feeling very hot and thirsty, I drank some and found it to be cool and good tasting.

No wonder the Indians used this island for a summer retreat. Everything they would possibly need was located at this precise spot. West Beach Cove with its bordering rocks would provide Mussels, Crabs, Clams, and other shellfish. The fishing of both fresh and salt water would be excellent. "Pig Nuts" grow a few inches deep in the soil. This wild vegetable, when cooked properly makes a very good porridge for breakfast. Of course, plenty of fresh water was available. Hickory nuts could be had a short distance away. There was plenty of sedge growing around the Lake to be used in constructing their summer wigwams. Birds are plentiful here. Some of them breed and have their young on the rocks surrounding the Lake. The Indians, as a change of pace, could catch some of the fowl and fetch the eggs for their eating pleasure. Hunting deer with bow and arrow, no doubt, was one of their favorite pastimes. But most importantly, this plot was well protected from the elements—an excellent site for an Indian summer village. It was even more so, I thought, an ideal place for seventeenth century English explorers to erect a fort and trading station.

Soon, I took a leisurely tour of the path walking south towards the natural sand deposit seen previously. Upon arrival, two deer were interrupted at their afternoon "happy hour". Standing at the bank and drinking, they straightened up at my coming and then fled quickly into the woods.

After a few minutes of scanning the terrain and taking a few pictures with my Minolta, I then proceeded to investigate the heavily wooded and rocky area close to the bank. Moving slowly and about twenty to thirty feet from the edge of the cliff, I made my way north. The going was rough. Twenty or so yards along, I stumbled into a small keetle hole or depression outlined with small boulders, a microscopic reminder of the Ice Age. Walking and sometimes crawling, I passed over many old rotted tree trunks and branches. Fighting my way through thorny briar I began to bleed from small cuts. Most of the trees were Beech and Oak with a scattering of Maple and Hop-Hornbeam. The soil was well mulched, in some places, with rotted leaves, wood, and other debris.

The rocks increased in size and numbers as I reached the highest point of the plot. They were all granitic and many were covered with pale green lichens. Already observed were two apparent clearings: That is, the spacing of the trees from each other suggested that the spot had been cleared at one time. At approximately the highest point of the islet which is thirty feet above sea level, the rocks were cut and fractured to a great extent. Some of them were cleaved at right angles, appearing to have been cut by man. Initially my imagination leapt, but was soon cooled by reason. The caution was based on experience as a teacher of the Earth Sciences. Many times while on field trips with my students, such phenomena were observed. The effect of the mastery of nature, sometimes, looks very much like the work of man. On the other hand, man might have a long way to go to imitate the artistry of nature.

From the highest point of the islet the land slopes downward. Still moving north, I entered a definite clearing a short distance away. This open area abutted the path and extended to the edge of the cliff. Its dimensions were roughly 38 yards by 32 yards. This space contained exactly four rocks, all about "kitchen table" size. One was shaped like a "V" which seemed interesting. There were only seven small trees. The tallest one measured 15 feet. The brush, beginning at the path, was one foot high and gradually increased to 5 feet at the edge of cliff.

Near the southern edge of the clearing a small hole was discovered shaped like a cigar. It was 15 feet long and about 3 feet wide. Grubbing and digging there with my bare hands, I found some fine smooth rocks that appeared to be beach stones. The question came to me: How were they transported from the beach a considerable distance off?

12

Because of my knowledge of early fort construction, familiarity with the Gosnold story, and the natural landscape of this spot, I wondered if I might not be standing on the site of Captain Gosnold's 1602 settlement. If rocks were needed for construction, they were readily available. Wood and sedge were also in abundance. The place had a commanding position and afforded good protection. In fact, the early colonizers were directed by their leaders to seek out areas like this for erecting small outposts. These stations would be initially used for trading purposes with the Indians and eventually as the forerunners of larger settlements.

I wondered how long it would take a person to reach this point from the apparent shoreline of the islet facing the swamp. I immediately walked straight across the path towards the beach. Upon entering the brush, I had to crawl on my hands and knees. Moving along, it occurred to me that I was following a deer trail. I reached the edge of the swamp in three minutes. Standing in a small clearing, I had a commanding view of the swamp and the cove beyond. I conjectured that it would have been a rather simple task to clear a path to the site I had just left.

I felt a sense of accomplishment, standing there. The wooded plot just explored seemed to fit the exact description given by Gosnold and his men of the islet in which they had built their fort. The size was the same, the vegetation, everything. Looking out over the heavy swamp and puddle-like stretch of water in its midst, I supposed that in 1602, this swamp was, in fact, an extension of the Pond. This thought further convinced me that I could well be standing near the first English habitation built on the shores of New England—a settlement that was the forerunner of Jamestown and Plymouth.

On my way back to the path, I wandered over to a somewhat smaller clearing that I had discovered in late August. It was located a few yards west of the path and within a stones throw of the clearing I was investigating. It had a soft grassy floor with some overhanging Maple tree branches blotting out the light. It was an excellent place to rest; so without hesitation, I stretched out on my back, completely exhausted. Soon, I began to chuckle, remembering my last visit to this spot in August.

During that visit, I had just finished a general survey of the rock formation near the cliff and was returning, in haste, to my boat, for it was near sunset. I was in a good mood, singing and shouting to myself as I blazed a trail through the bramble. I had not shaved for days and was wearing a yellow kerchief around my forehead, black swimming trunks, and a red shirt. In my right hand, I was swinging a machete, bought recently in an Army-Navy store. This was a very useful tool for travelling through bush country. I suppose I looked like some kind of pirate, brought back from the dead.

Screaming the lyrics of *"Yo ho ho and a bottle of rum on a dead man's chest,"* I burst into the clearing of soft grass. There, before me, were two startled people: one male and one female. They were huddled together near a small campfire with their mouths wide open in disbelief and possibly horror. Partly clad and, I guessed, somewhere in their early twenties, they evidently had just crawled out of the sleeping bag lying nearby. The girl was attempting to hide what could have been the result of a love engagement within the bag. The boy had a good size rock in his hand ready to protect his maiden fair, and hurtle it at this monster of the woods.

I towered over them, and pointing to the campfire with my machete said: "There are no open fires allowed on this island. Please, in all haste, put the damn thing out." Without answering, they nodded their heads and quickly threw some sand on the fire. I, then, dashed into the woods to my boat.

I suppose that they later might have told their friends of the experience, pointing out that if one does dirty deeds on this island like throwing away beer cans, making indiscriminate love, or molesting anything that belongs there, a terrible creature will appear and threaten. If no heed is taken from the warning, the creature will cut off heads with his blood stained machete. Who knows, maybe I started a new legend on the islands.

The thought of that August episode seemed to rejuvenate me. I now felt that I had enough stamina for the return trip to the farmhouse. The walk to the west of the island was slow but without pain or affliction. I arrived there just as the now exposed sun was setting. Standing on the shore of Robinson's Hole, I looked across to Pasque Island. There were some flickering lights from two of the houses and I saw smoke spiralling from the chimneys. I also noticed a power boat anchored a short distance from the island's shore and supposed that the Forbes duck hunting party was bedding down for the night.

14

Completely worn out, I entered my outermost house and built a small fire with kindling and pieces of log which were conveniently placed for my use. I lighted a small hurricane lamp and prepared supper consisting of cold beans, horseradish, two aspirins, and about five ounces of that good Russian beverage. I ate and drank with relish, then sat down finally, on a worn sofa facing the fireplace. I had planned to review my notes but decided to wait until morning.

I picked up my E. B. White and William Strunk's *Elements of Style* and made an attempt to read. Soon I was drifting off to sleep.

Chapter Three

FOREVER RADIANT

And looking on this lustrous spot below,
In morn's creation-burst, or sunset's glow,
This little heaven of beauty, peace, and love,
Who could forget the kindred heaven above?

E. S. W.
Verses From The Island
Book, 1865

The next morning I awoke at about 4 A.M. After a few minutes of lying in bed, collecting my thoughts on the up-coming activities, a short breakfast consisting of the remaining beans and some horseradish was consumed. I washed the food down with very cold water taken from the manual pump located in the kitchen. After breakfast, I walked to the shore of Robinson's Hole and washed my mouth with seawater, an excellent substitute for a dentifrice.

Back in the house, I began to study the topographic map and the notes of the previous day. Everything still seemed to corroborate my assumption that I might have in fact, located the true site of Captain Gosnold's installation. Why might Elizabethan Adventurers not have seen, as had I, how natural a spot this was for a fort? The wooded plot at the Pond was protected, convenient, and possessed the necessary elements for life support.

It was not difficult to decide my schedule. I would, first, take some pictures of the Westend Pond area and then leave for the east end of the island at about 10 A.M. Since I had no watch and the ferry left at 4 P.M., the schedule would have to be well organized. This was one boat I did not want to miss. I thought six hours would be sufficient for the seven mile trek, with brief excursions here and there off the beaten track.

At 7 A.M. I hastily gathered my equipment and prepared to leave. With the knapsack on my back and a long handled spade

16

shovel over the shoulder I began the long hike, leaving the quahog rake behind to lessen the load. No short cuts through thorny bushes for me, this time. I stayed on the bridal path, shown on the map, and reached the Pond within a half-an-hour. As I stood on some high ground overlooking the Pond at the south side, I muttered:

"Da Yo Ha Gwenda",

the Wampanoag Indian phrase meaning "an opening in the woods". The Wampanoags had used the island for a place of repose. In fact, a probable Indian translation of Naushon is, "the Spirit of God". I thought to myself that, God willing, this beautiful Pond will, hopefully, always be used as a great resting place, a spot where one can meditate among natural surroundings, a true opening in the woods for people, especially those with troubled spirits.

In less than two hours, the picture taking was completed. At about midmorning with a brilliant sun and hazy blue sky overhead, I prepared to embark on my miniature Odyssey. But just as I began my race with time to the east end of Naushon, I had an unexpected human visitor.

A lady on horseback came trotting towards me from the north. We met near the little stone bridge on the north side of the islet near the Pond. Surprised, I greeted her with a hearty hello. She introduced herself as Mrs. David Forbes, wife of Naushon's owner, explaining that she was doing her usual Sunday morning routine of "riding the island". Knowing why I was there, she inquired about my success. I told her that things went well and that I might even have found the site of Captain Gosnold's fort, pointing to the general direction of the clearing I had explored the previous day. Seemingly surprised and pleased, she offered me a red, rosy apple for my reward. I immediately accepted it and, even more promptly, consumed the fruit in her presence. It was probably not good manners, but I was hungry. Beans, chop suey and horseradish are not a sufficient diet for a man with a Lithuanian ancestry.

After a short interval of small talk, we wished each other a good day and went our separate ways, I towards the east and she to the west.

I reached Crescent Beach, shortly. Here the seagulls breed on the rocks. Leaning against one of these rocks, I studied the topographic map with a magnifying glass to determine the course to Hadley Harbor. Taking into account that it was then around 11 A.M., I had five hours to reach my destination. I decided to travel the path called the Main Road which runs along the northern side of the island. At times, this path wanders to the north shore, especially near Kettle Cove, halfway up the island. Past the Cove, I would follow Memory Road to Mt. Cary near Silver Beach. From that point, I would explore the interior taking the path to Mt. Surat, the highest point on the island. The rest of the journey would be down hill, so to speak, with only a two mile stretch of heavy woods to tramp before reaching the Forbes' Mansions near Hadley Harbor.

The brilliant October sun was at my back as I set out again. I had the binoculars around my neck and the boyscout compass in my pocket for instant use. The knapsack, now containing forty pounds of assorted equipment was securely fastened to my back. The long handle spade shovel was used for a walking stick.

Within a few thousand feet of Crescent Beach, I encountered several sheep grazing among tall grass and shrubs. As I came close to them, some ran into the woods. However, a few stood their ground and stared at me. Their almost human-like "bah" seemed to imply that my presence was enjoyed and that they were giving me a warm greeting. They are allowed absolute freedom and are only molested once a year when their coats are removed.

Walking in a northeast direction, I shortly entered the Ramshead Woods, a forest of Beech trees with some scattered Oak both black and white. Also seen was a lone Holly tree, far in the woods to my right. Later I noticed some small Black Cherry trees, many varieties of Dogwood, and a few Red Cedar. The ground cover consisted of Ferns, Parsley, and Sedge, in the lower spots. Tansy and Pinesap dominated the higher ground. Of course, in many places, there was the ever-present Bullbrier and other thorny bushes and vines. The foliage was generally past its peak, the leaves showing their lucid yellows and pale reds, with a splash of crimson in the swampy areas.

There was no evidence that man had ever been here. The place was completely in solitude. These beautiful surroundings around me, which compared to the *Garden of Eden,* seemed to convey a message of total preservation. If the island of Naushon

18

could speak, it probably would say: "I exist for all people. Please don't sin upon me."

In 1602, the English explorers found that when they planted Wheat, Barley and Oats on Naushon, the seeds sprang up over nine inches in fourteen days in "fat and lusty" soil. I tested the soil, once, and found it to be of sandy loam, grayish in color, about eight inches deep. I suppose the explorers must have planted on the east end of the island where the ground is richer. Grubbing around with my hands, a string of "Pig Nuts" was found about three inches deep in the ground. They have a tannish color on the outside and some of them look very much like hens' eggs. They are linked together and there may be at least a dozen of them on a string. They are good to eat and taste not unlike potatoes when cooked with salt, butter, and milk, and garnished with some red onion and paprika.

In about an hour I was out of the woods and standing on a plain, overlooking Kettle Cove. I sat on a rock and looked at Buzzards Bay. The visibility was excellent. I could easily see the Dartmouth, Massachusetts shore some twelve miles to the north. The far shoreline bends like a bow from southwest to northeast and then east. All was quiet and there were no boats of any kind in the Cove, only the sand, rocks, and me. The prominent head-land of Rams Head was about 1000 feet to my west. Its sparkling cliff, forty feet high presented a bullish face of rock and gravel. One can walk out to its grassy top and see almost the entire shore-line of Buzzards Bay; from Dartmouth in a circular direction to West Falmouth, Massachusetts.

I fixed my eyes on a particularly large boulder, sitting near the base of the cliff in about ten feet of water. Millions of years ago it was not resting there but was in a liquid form thousands of feet below the surface of the earth. Then it oozed to the surface and hardened fast; probably where New Hampshire now is located. Then 10,000 years ago, a mass of ice, thousands of feet thick, scooped it up and pushed it farther south, and now it stands there in the Cove. Underneath its homely brown and gray surface are found Garnet and Rose Quartz that gleam with a radiant luster. It is a gem of nature, untapped.

I pushed myself away from my resting place, turned my back on the "virgin" rock near the cliff, and in a rather subdued and tranquil mood headed back into the forest. Although the little

19

compass assured me that I was travelling more or less easterly, and the topographic map pointed out the paths clearly, sometimes it was confusing because of the winding and melding together of these "roads". For example, shortly after leaving Kettle Cove, I faced a crossroad with three paths all heading in an easterly direction. The one desired was called Memory Road, but there were no street signs around to help me. I selected the one that seemed to run more due east than the other two. Fortunately, it turned out to be the correct choice, and my pace quickened, involuntarily. Perhaps the subconscious was reminding me that it was around high noon, and I had five or so miles yet to walk.

One particular feature about the woods is worth mentioning. Upon entering a depression or kettle hole, the trees were found in greater numbers and growing closer together. However, as I would approach the crest of any one of these holes or small valleys, the trees would be fewer in number or, in some cases, non-existent. In fact, the taller trees are found at the bottom of these ravines. The trees then, become progressively shorter in height as one reaches the top of a hill. I suspect the reason for this phenonema is that extensive vegetation cannot easily flourish where exposed to the full force of the wind. For example, Cutty-hunk, an island with grassy meadows and low rolling hills, is almost completely exposed to the prevailing winds from the south-west. As a result, no substantial tree growth is found on the island. On Naushon, however, with its many deep hollows, there is a profusion of plant life of great variety, for the simple reason that this island affords more protection from the elements.

Another interesting feature was the spacing of the trees from each other. Many times during the walk, I could see a furlong in all directions, although surrounded on all sides with heavy forest growth. This resulted in a very fascinating scene. Beams of solid sunlight, intercepted by clusters of multi-colored leaves, produced a picture of nature that seemed almost artificial.

Being hungry, tired, and thirsty, and on schedule with Mt. Cary only three-quarters of a mile distant, I sat down on the ground to rest awhile. To satisfy my thirst, since there was no drinking water, I placed a small Hickory nut in my mouth. I remembered, while at college, the Cross-Country runners used to put a small pebble in their mouths. This procedure would activate the salivary glands and temporarily eliminate the want for water while running long distances. The nut, one of hundreds at my feet, produced the same effect. After a few minutes of sucking on the nut, I cracked it open and tasted the meat. It was very good. Several more were opened and consumed. After the lunch of Hickory nuts and saliva, I grabbed my long handled spade shovel, lifted myself upright, and moved on.

I soon came upon exceedingly green grassy ground with few if any trees, crisscrossed with fieldstone walls. One or two of these rocky borders run north and south almost the entire width of the island. Although it seemed I was in the midst of cattle grazing country, no cows were seen. Near an old gate that led into one of the pastures I noticed an old sign posted on a pole that read: "Beware Of The Bull". Curious, because there was not a bull in sight, I climbed a knoll which had a commanding position of the immediate area. Some three hundred yards distant, I thought I saw a large black creature. However, with the aid of my binoculars it was found to be only an illusion. This apparition was actually a small clump of Bayberry, partially shaded by a large rock.

Suddenly, there was a loud thrashing in the bush behind me. Fearful, I turned quickly. For a fleeting moment, I saw three miniature deer dash away. Thankful that there would be no fight with a bull that day, I continued my journey eastward.

Later, I remembered that those deer were about two feet tall and appeared to be adult animals, pigmy deer, so to speak. A few years ago I read somewhere that a former owner of Naushon brought these animals to the island where they now thrive.

In a short time Mt. Cary, a hill with an elevation of 120 feet, was reached. From its peak, I could see Mt. Surat, only one half mile further east. Mt. Surat, according to the map, is the highest point on the island with an elevation of 160 feet. It also has a steep gradiant or relief which makes it appear higher. Without resting, I made my way to Mt. Surat where I planned to take a fifteen minute siesta, for the sun was past its zenith, indicating that it was about one o'clock in the afternoon. When the summit was reached, I removed my pea jacket and placed the knapsack on the ground. I then stood erect, facing the cooling breeze from the northwest. The visibility was unlimited with only a thin whispy haze over the distant shoreline. A quarter-of-mile from Naushon's northern shore lay the small Weepecket Isles. These islands are barren and broken pieces of land. The largest of the group, only a half-mile in circumference, was called a "white headed eagle" by the Indians. To me, it looked like a badly mangled one, with its broken rocky bones split and shattered by wind and waves. Most of its original area now makes a submerged ledge extending towards the Falmouth, Massachusetts coast.

The emerald green and silvery blue water of Buzzards Bay was sparkling in the sunlight. The shore to the north, some fifteen miles distant, seemed much closer because of the clear atmosphere. To the east was a two-mile expanse of very dense forest that contained almost every type of tree one could possibly identify in New England: young Sassafras with leaves yellow and green, Red Maple and Black Gum, the umbrella-like Hop-Hornbeam with its crazy crooked stem, Witch Hazel with their pea shaped blue and bitter nuts, Orange and Velvety Oak, also Red and White Cedar with scattered Black Cherry, and now and then a glistening green Holly. The ever green spines of the Pitch Pine and the late turning leaves of the Dogwoods melded well with the fast-changing foliage of the other trees, now yellow, brown and red.

Just beyond the forest were the many small islands of Naushon, loosely connected to each other and protecting Hadley Harbor within. Nonamesset and Uncatena with the scattered islets called Monahansett, Cedar, Goats, Bucks, and Bulls, presented a vivid picture of what John Brereton, companion of Bartholomew Gosnold, described in 1602:

> It [Naushon] conteineth many pieces or necks of land, which differ nothing from several islands, saving that certain banks of small breadth do like bridges join them to this island. [1]

Across the passage that separates the islands from the mainland stood Woods Hole, Massachusetts, with its unique assortment of people. Philosophers, scientists, educators, wandering freaks and middle Americans all live there. The buildings of the Oceanographic Institution, the Bureau of Commercial Fisheries, and the Marine Biological Laboratory are intermingled with elegant homes and native shops. An infinitesimal speck of what is called Civilization.

[1] John Brereton, *A Briefe and true Relation of the Discoverie of the North part of Virginia* . . . (2nd ed., London: George Bishop, 1602).

Across Vineyard Sound to the south, I could see the entire island of Capawack, alias Martha's Vineyard, twenty-five miles of sandy beaches, rolling tree-covered hills, and staggering bluffs.

Anxious to complete my Odyssey, I walked down, and down, to a place called Eagle Hollow. I went from daylight to darkness, into the shade of the forest. In the midst of this captivating wood, I felt very tired and lay down under a small Maple tree. I fell asleep instantly and had a soft uninterrupted nap that must have lasted at least an hour. When I awoke and saw that the sun was sinking fast in the west, I covered the last mile of my journey in almost a sprint, scattering some red-necked Turkeys that crossed the path on the way. I arrived at Hadley Harbor at 4 P.M.

I boarded the ferry for home and turned my back on Naushon: a place where one could draw his mantle around him and find romance.

Chapter Four

THANKSGIVING, 1602 STYLE

Here are we sit beneath the deepening shade
And muse upon the Indian's hapless fate,
While twilight spreads o'er all her dusky veil,
The memories that linger round these scenes
Are of the sacred, precious things of earth,
And lift our hearts in gratitude to Him,
Alike the Indian's and the white man's God.

W. W. S.
Verses From The Island
Book, 1865

Before the white man came to America, the Indians called Naushon, *Kataymuck.* This word, with its various spellings, has the following definitions: The great spring or planting place; the great fishing place; or the crab fishing place. All three definitions of the word fit the island very well even today.

Blue Crabs roam the bottom of Robinson's Hole between Pasque and Naushon. Scampering Green Crabs are found under almost every rock along the shoreline. A short distance offshore, a fisherman has his choice of catching Blues, Stripers or the many variety of ground fish, such as Scup and Flounder. The soil, as was mentioned previously, is good, especially at the east end of the island. In the summer months the Indians would prepare small plots of squash, beans, and corn to help supplement their diet of seafood.

But the English, intent on colonization, wanted the island for their own use. In 1641, Thomas Mayhew, an English missionary, bought Martha's Vineyard from his countrymen. Also included in the deal was the right to purchase Naushon from the Indians. However, Mayhew had a problem figuring out which Indian owned the island because so many sub-tribes of the Wampanoag nation took advantage of its resources for a summer camping site. May-

24

hew solved this dilemma by having several Sachems or Chiefs make their mark on a deed of ownership, an arrangement which cost him one pound of gunpowder and an unknown quantity of shot. In 1557, Mayhew collected his deed, satisfied that he finally had full ownership of the island:

This is to witness that I Quaquaquinigat Sachem have for ever sold for me my heirs and assigns the Island of Kattymuck to Thomas Mayhew of Martha's Vineyard for him his heirs and assigns to enjoy forever without interruption of me or any of my posterity witness my hand this thirteenth day of August one thousand six hundred fifty and seven [1657] and do hereby acknowledge to have received of said Thomas Mayhew two coats in full satisfaction for the same, witnesseth also here to my hand this year and day aforesaid. [2]

To say the Indians were robbed is a gross understatement: In 1950, the total real estate valuation of the Elizabeth Islands was the impressive sum of $1,273,690.00. Naushon, with its sub-islands alone, was valued at $653,202.00. There is no question that the islands are worth much more today. On the other hand, one could say that these islands are priceless and never should be sold again for money. No doubt, the "giving" of Naushon to the English by the Indians for two coats and some ammunition was simply a token gesture on their part. They assumed that they would continue to use and enjoy the islands forever, as had been their previous custom.

The first recorded meeting between the English and the Indians on Naushon was a delightful, if not significantly remarkable experience. It took place in early June of 1602, some eighteen years before Plymouth. In fact, it definitely was the first recorded "clambake" held on the shores of New England. On 31 May, Captain Gosnold, with a Longboat full of men, crossed Buzzards Bay from Naushon and landed just outside New Bedford Harbor. A reception committee of Indians greeted the English. The atmosphere was kind and courteous. The "first Americans" presented to Captain Gosnold such items as hemp, animal furs, copper trinkets, and tobacco. The whitemen were somewhat embarrassed since they had nothing to offer in return, but the Indians didn't seem to be insulted and said they would come over to Naushon in a few days to return the visit. The Adventurers went back to Naushon and fell in with their labors of building the fort and collecting Sassafras for their cargo home.

[2] Deeds of Ownership, County of Dukes County in Massachusetts, Edgartown, Massachusetts.

A few days later, the Chief, probably Massasoit's father or Massasoit himself, with some of his subordinates, came to Naushon and visited the English briefly. He pointed to the Sun, a sign meaning that he would return the next day.

Early the next morning, the Adventurers sighted nine canoes carrying fifty Indians crossing the Bay. The natives landed on the island some distance from the fort. An English party of twenty men, with Gabriel Archer as leader, went out to greet them. All of the Indians were armed with bows and arrows. This sight worried Archer since Captain Gosnold, with most of the arms, was three miles away, aboard *Concord*. If the Indians decided to attack, he and his men would not stand a chance. Visions of the "Lost Colony" of Roanoke, supposedly massacred by an Indian attack, must have flashed through his mind.

His apprehension was quickly dispelled, however. As he approached the Indians, holding his musket in a rather threatening manner, the Chief lay down his weapons in a sign of peace. Archer, relieved, did likewise. The two leaders then embraced each other. At once, all fifty Indians sat around in a circle like greyhounds with the Chief in their midst. Both sides began to mingle and exchange gifts; the Indians offered their furs of beaver, black fox, seal, deer, and otter, and the English gave shining beads and knives.

Meanwhile, Captain Gosnold had arrived on the scene. His company, heralding his coming, set up two lines of officers with muskets at arms. The brave sea captain walked between the honor guard and saluted the Chief with great respect. He then presented the "Lord Commander" of all present-day Southeastern Massachusetts and part of Rhode Island a straw hat and a pair of knives. Gabriel Archer wrote later:

. . . the hat awhile he wore, but the knives, he beheld with great marvelling, being very bright and sharp; this our courtesy made them all in love with us. [3]

After the formal opening exercises, the two groups spent the rest of the day chatting and trading. John Brereton later recalled:

They pronounce our language with great facilitie [ease]; for one of them, one day sitting by me, upon occasion I spake smiling to him these words: "How now (sirha) are you so saucie with my tobacco?" which words (without any further repetition) he suddenly spake so plaine and distinctly, as if he had been a long scholar in the language. [4]

[3] Gabriel Archer, *The Relation of Captaine Gosnols Voyage to the North Part of Virginia* in Samuel Purchas, *Purchas His Pilgrims* (London, 1625), V, 1647-51.
[4] *Brereton Relation.*

The English considered copper a very valuable commodity and were surprised to find many of the Indians adorned with it in the form of chains and bracelets. Brereton wrote:

They have also great store of Copper, some very redde, and some of a paler colour . . . yet I was desireous to understand where they had such store of this metall, and made signs to one of them (with whom I was very familiar) who taking a piece of copper in his hand, made a hole with his finger in the ground, and with all, pointed to the main from whence he came. [5]

Brereton might have been disappointed, however, if he had decided to try to find some of this metal. The Indian, to be sure, was pointing in the general direction of copper mines, but they probably were located in what is now central New York state, a long 300 to 400 mile walk for an English gentleman adventurer.

Towards evening, the Indians retreated to their campsite three or four miles away, possibly on Pasque Island. On the next morning, the sixth of June, everyone was disappointed for it was raining and it continued to pour all day. So, the planned festivities were postponed until the following day.

The next morning, Indians and whitemen worked together in preparing the feast scheduled for noon. Fires were set near the beach. The English cooked mutton and pork, and garnished it with mustard. Plenty of beer was on hand. The Indians busied themselves roasting crabs and herring. They also broiled a great amount of ground nuts. Sassafras tea was available for those who refrained from taking alcoholic beverages. Plenty of tobacco was available to both parties for an after dinner smoke. At noon, dinner was served; and the small representative gathering of two alien cultures sat down in a circle and enjoyed the food in an atmosphere of thanksgiving.

This band of Wampanoag Indians, in 1602, could have wiped out the visitors with ease. Their people were strong and healthy. They often waged war with their neighbors the Narragansetts. In fact, in previous times, it is reported that the natives had waylaid fishing vessels that wandered too close to the coast and then captured and killed the whitemen, taking their cargo and belongings. It is not well known that the Indians of New England were excellent sailors. The case was quite different in 1620, however. Disease had weakened the population, resulting in a considerable loss of life. As a matter of fact Massasoit more than welcomed

[5] Ibid.

27

the Pilgrims because he thought that they might provide him medical assistance and other aid for his people.

One wonders what changes would have occurred in our history if Bartholomew Gosnold had successfully established a permanent colony in New England. His calm temperament and his deep regard for the Indians and their land is shown in the reports of the visit. Gosnold, who five years later become a "prime mover" of the first permanent English colony at Jamestown, Virginia in 1607, deserves more credit in our history books, for he "opened the door" of English colonization in America. Where is the New England conscience?

The feast lasted most of the afternoon, but not without a hitch. One of the Indians apparently overcome by the beer, stole a shield from the English. Captain Gosnold, when informed of the act by one of his crew, drew the attention of the Chief to this fact. The Chief immediately had the thief apprehended and the shield was restored with apologetic comments from both sides. Late in the day, when the Indians prepared to depart, the Chief left a few of his warriors behind to help the English dig Sassafras. Thus ended the first real "Thanksgiving" ever held on the shores of New England. John Brereton recorded the closing ceremonies thusly:

. . . but being in their canoes a little from the shore, they made huge cries and shouts of joy unto us; and we with our trumpet and cornet and casting up our cappes into the aire, made them the best farewell we could. [6]

[6] Ibid.

Chapter Five

ROMANCE RUNNETH ALL OVER THE PLACE

Then here be thoughtful: reverently tread
Where slumber unrecorded dead.
Loving and lived, mourning and mourned,
Have made this consecrated ground.
The Past is here: there is no spot
Of this fair Isle it hollows not.

L. F. B.
Verses From The Island
Book, 1865

When Wait Winthrop bought Naushon in 1682, he said that it was an "extraordinary thing for the price". Even more remarkable are the several episodes involving the maritime history of the island. One can even speculate not idly I think, that there was a strong connection between Shakespeare and the island, that it was indeed the basis for his play The Tempest first produced in London in 1610 (See Appendix B).

On 27 August 1689, the notorious pirate, Thomas Pound, pursued the brigantine *Merrimack* into Vineyard Haven Harbor on Martha's Vineyard and robbed her of provisions. This being one of many such escapades by this pirate, up and down the New England coast, the British authorities had had enough. They sent out Captain Samuel Pease with Lieutenant Benjamin Gallup as second officer in the sloop *Mary*. *Mary's* orders were to track down Pound and bring him back dead or alive. In late September and early October of 1689, the *Mary* and the Pirate vessel engaged in a fierce battle off Tarpoulin Cove at Naushon.

Upon sighting the pirate ship, Captain Pease ordered the King's Jack raised to the masthead. As she overhauled the pirates, the *Mary* fired her great gun. Immediately, the outlaw ship responded by raising the red flag of piracy, and at close quarters the battle commenced. After the ships exchanged sev-

29

eral volleys of musket fire for about an hour, Captain Pease shouted across to the pirates, "Strike for the King of England."

Captain Pound, standing on his quarter deck and flashing his naked sword, retorted, angrily, "Come aboard you dogs and I will strike you presently."

The two ships then renewed their musket firing with greater intensity. Soon *Mary* managed to leeward of the *Pirate,* a distinct advantage because of a brisk wind. Suddenly, two kegs of gunpowder exploded on the *Mary,* severely wounding two men. Assuming that the government ship was in deep trouble, the pirates cheered and then increased their firing.

Captain Pease screamed, "We will give you quarter if you will surrender."

The pirates responded, "No, we will give *you* quarter, if *you* surrender."

The battle continued to rage on. Two more government sailors were wounded. Captain Pease, himself, caught a musket ball in the chest and was carried below. Lieutenant Gallup, now in command, managed to steer the *Mary* alongside the *Pirate.* What followed was several minutes of hand to hand combat that must have equalled, if not surpassed, any such scene in a Hollywood movie. The British sailors swarmed aboard the pirate ship with blazing sabers and barking hand guns. Bare fists smashed against bearded chins. It was a gory struggle. The deck of the ship was, literally drenched with blood and parts of bodies and entrails from both sides. Pound, himself and only one of his crew still standing, finally surrendered. Twelve pirates were wounded and four lay dead on the deck. Captain Pease died of his wounds as the *Mary* made her way to Boston.

Captain Pound was never brought to trial. One reason might be that the wife of the Governor of the colony was a sister to Thomas Hawkins, an associate of Pound. This suggests that Pound had political influence within the government.

Another "pirate" who had little political pull, especially near the end of his career, was Captain William Kidd. Kidd's connection with Naushon is rather cloudy. No doubt he used Tarpoulin Cove as a watering place for his vessels on several occasions but not as a pirate. Some authorities, even today, are skeptical about the validity of the pirate designation attached to his name. Captain Kidd was a privateer, in other words, one who had permission of the British government to seek out and capture vessels of any country it disliked. The privateer would bring his "prize" back to port and divide the profit with his crew. Of course, the government would take its share; a very legal and sometimes lucrative business in those days.

Kidd had a good reputation as a mariner and organizer. In 1696, he was commissioned by the British to destroy a pirate fleet in the Indian Ocean which was harassing their merchant ships there. On 6 September 1696, he sailed from his home port of New York in command of *Adventure Galley* with 74 guns and 155 men. The entire operation was a complete disaster and resulted in his eventual trial on piracy charges. No pirates were captured on this expedition. There even were reports that Kidd attacked several vessels flying his own country's flag. At no time during the trip, however, did he fly the red flag of piracy. His crew was often mutinous, and in one incident, Kidd, in a fit of rage, killed one of his officers in cold blood. Disease and starvation also plagued this miserable adventure. Complaints of Kidd's shady activities were officially filed in London by the British East India Company, and orders were sent out to apprehend him as a pirate and murderer.

On the voyage home, Kidd managed to escape capture. Leaving his ship at a West Indian island, he loaded a small sloop with all of his captured booty including some precious stones and gold. He then successfully sailed up the eastern coast of the present-day United States, arriving in New York in 1699. After a short stay at his home in New York City with his wife and child, he again sailed along the coast to Boston. On route, he stopped at Gardner Island in Long Island Sound and buried some of his "treasure." He also payed a brief visit to the innkeeper at Tarpoulin Cove on Naushon.

Soon after his arrival in Boston, he was arrested and sent to England for trial on charges of piracy on the high seas and murder. His trial was held in the spring of 1700, on what some authorities claim were "trumped-up charges." Generally speaking, the trial was an unfair one by today's standards. Kidd steadfastly argued that he was innocent of all accusations and often exploded in a rage while in court. His nasty temperament certainly did not help his predicament. The result was inevitable. On 23 May 1701,

31

Captain William Kidd of New York was hanged for murder and for piracy against the King of England.

When Kidd arrived in Boston from New York, the authorities quickly recovered his buried loot on Gardner Island. However, they were not certain that they had the entire booty. When questioned, Kidd said nothing. It is often supposed that he might have hidden the remaining loot at one of the Elizabeth Islands, perhaps at Tarpoulin Cove on Naushon.

Despite Kidd's connection with the Cape Cod area, the only monument found today in his name is the Captain Kidd Restaurant in Woods Hole, Massachusetts, a place where, sometimes, modern-day pirates, of shorts, hang out.

During the War of Independence, Tarpoulin Cove was a favorite haunt for British naval vessels. The innkeeper there, Elisha Nye, seemed to play "musical chairs" in his dealings with the enemy. In the spring of 1775, the *HMS Faulkland,* after a raid on the Elizabeth Islands, anchored at Tarpoulin Cove. When the Captain came ashore with some armed men, the women of the Inn immediately fled into the woods. The Captain approached Nye and said, "Don't be afraid, we mean no harm," and demanded an inventory of the innkeeper's stock and provisions. Satisfied with Nye's report that he had only a number of sheep, he said, "If you sell anything to the rebels, I will take the rest by force."

Nye responded, "Yes sir; the sheep are thin, now, but when they are fat I will sell them to you."

Many of the Islanders, especially those of Nantucket, were sympathetic towards the British; perhaps they were just trying to save their own skins.

The British carried out many raids on Naushon; one of them, similar to the "Concord Bridge" affair, met considerable resistance. The British Men of War, *HMS Diamond* and *HMS Ambuscade,* were lying in wait off Tarpoulin Cove on 12 December 1776 with orders to intercept and destroy rebel privateers. Some of the British officers, led by Captain Fielding, came ashore with a flag of truce to purchase supplies from the innkeeper. They were immediately fired upon by a dozen patriots hiding behind the rocks. One of the officers received a musket ball through the head. The British vessels off shore opened fire

32

with their big guns, and 140 marines, promptly stormed the beach. They received heavy volleys of shot from the Americans but managed to drive them to the other side of the island. The patriots made their escape over Buzzards Bay in small boats but not without some casualties. Five Americans were killed in the engagement. One British marine lost his life and two were wounded.

One of the most daring encounters between the Americans and the British occurred during the War of 1812. Captain Weston Jenkins of Falmouth with thirty-two men aboard the sloop, *Two Friends,* captured a British privateer off Naushon on the night of 18 October 1814. The *Two Friends* drifted towards the privateer in a still night with light rain falling. The British privateer, *Retaliation,* anchored in Tarpoulin Cove, sent out a barge to intercept the sloop and then fired a warning shot across her bow. The barge approached the sloop and the officer in command demanded surrender. The British saw only Captain Jenkins and a few others on deck. However, when the Englishmen came alongside, twenty Americans stood up from below the gunnels with muskets pointed at the enemy. Captain Jenkins and his crew then took over the barge, towing the sloop with the captives aboard towards the *Retaliation.* With ease and without resistance, they boarded the privateer and captured the surprised British crew. Captain Jenkins sailed the *Retaliation* back to Falmouth as a prize of war.

The story of Naushon, to be sure, is a glittering one. But this queenly island also has her ladies of court that form the chain of the Elizabeths: Pasque, Nashawena, Cuttyhunk, and Penikese have their stories too.

33

Chapter Six

THE OFFSPRING SHAPED LIKE A DOME

The sea broke through,
Forming you:
A crab-strewn coast,
Nature's host.

Harold C. Wilson
1973

While Gosnold and his men were building their fort in the late spring of 1602, Naushon was giving birth to a daughter isle. Her name would later become Pasque; her father was the wind and the waves. Today, Pasque is separated from its mother by the narrow channel known as Robinson's Hole. The natural afterbirth of submerged rocks and boulders produces whirling currents, which make the place a very treacherous passage for sailing craft. The Indian meaning of Pasque is "where the sea breaks through." This translation is supported by Gabriel Archer in his description of Naushon on 28 May 1602:

This island in the western side admitteth some in creeks or sandy coves, so girded, as the water in some places of each side meeteth, to which the Indians of the main do often resort for fishing of crabs. [7]

Pasque is one-and-three-quarters of a mile long and one-mile wide. It has no trees to speak of. In its exposed central region which is constantly weathered by the elements, boulders, large and small, dominate. From its highest point, the land gradually recedes to the shoreline, giving Pasque a dome-like appearance. As a result there are no high bluffs on the shore but mostly rock strewn beaches providing excellent bathing areas, especially on the west end, facing Quick's Hole. On the east end there is a winding in-creek penetrating through an extensive low and marshy area. The creek provides an excellent harbor for small boats, and it is here that the only buildings on the island are located.

[7] Archer Relation.

34

An old farmhouse, still in excellent condition, sits on a hill-side overlooking Robinson's Hole. No one knows for sure when it was built. Some people think it goes back to the early seventeenth century. In fact, a legend claims that some of Gosnold's men returned to the Elizabeth Islands around 1615 and built the house. If the legend is true, a possible answer might be found with the Tucker family of Dartmouth, Massachusetts, just outside New Bedford. Descendants of the early Tuckers, who once owned the island, still reside in the New Bedford area. It is known that Archer, recorder of the Gosnold voyage, named a Cape Cod shoal, *Tucker's Terror*. It is also known that Gosnold's men thought highly of the Elizabeth Islands. Although a man named Tucker, no doubt, was with Gosnold in 1602, we don't know anything more about him. There is a good possibility that he was a Daniel Tucker who followed Gosnold to Jamestown, Virginia in 1608. Heirs of this Tucker eventually bought Pasque Island.

Geologically, Pasque is similar to Naushon, but is unlike the mother in vegetation, being almost completely barren. Its many swampy areas on the southeast, south, and west side are screened with Huckleberry, Bayberry and other similar bushes. Wild Rose or "Rose Hip" is plentiful and provides a distinct sweet aroma for the nearby beaches, especially during the early summer months. The fruit of this Rose bush is edible. When ripe, it looks like a miniature tomato and has a "tangy" taste. One must be careful when eating one to nibble only on the outer part, as a rabbit gnaws a carrot. The center of the fruit is somewhat bitter and contains numerous tiny seeds that do not add to its eating enjoyment. Several times, I have prepared a "Rose Hip Salad" which I call "The John Crosby Brown Experience", in honor of a former owner of Pasque who greatly appreciated the island. The salad consists of one-inch sections of slightly cooked Chicken's Feet — a small edible plant, not unlike asparagus in appearance, which grows on the outer perimeter of salt marshes — finely chopped Pig Weed, which has a sour taste; and, of course, plenty of raw Rose Hip fruit carefully cut in quarters with the seeds removed. This recipe, gently seasoned with a red wine vinegar and olive oil dressing, goes very well with all kinds of seafood dishes.

Although the Elizabeth Islands, as noted previously, were practically stolen from the Indians in the mid 1600's, a small group of natives managed, in 1667, to recover some of their losses. The incident occurred at the west end of Pasque Island.

35

Early in the morning on 22 November 1667, a vessel loaded with cargo was driven by a violent tempest onto the west shore of Pasque Island, facing Quick's Hole. The crew managed to wade ashore and warm themselves at an Indian hut. Soon, some Indians arrived and without hesitation, declared that the stricken ship with all its supplies was rightfully theirs. The alarmed white men protested angrily. After several minutes of arguing back and forth, the Indians finally told the crew and their captain to leave the hut while they had a powwow with their Chief. About an hour later the Indians informed the white men that they would take the vessel and all she possessed. Despite futile protests from the crew, the Indians carried off everything from the ship leaving the crew only the clothes on their back and a little food. The following is a complete list of the items taken:

> The Captain's personal gear including one suit of clothes, two pairs of shoes, all of his tools, a new hat and his son's brand new shoes.
> The vessel of 15 tons capacity, including its furniture and an extra foresail, cables and anchor.
> 48 liters of Indian corn.
> 4 barrels of pork.
> 4 animal hides.
> Some butter.
> One small cask of suett.
> One barrel of tobacco.
> About 34 liters of cotton.
> 26 bushels of meal.
> 2 bushels of turnip.
> One bushel of onions.
> 6 yards of red cloth.
> One pair of worn shoes.
> 2 iron pots.
> 3 pairs of children's shoes.
> A barrel of tarrow.
> 2 guns.
> One green blanket.
> One woman's cloak.

It is not known if the Indians were prosecuted for what could be called an act of piracy, but it could also be argued that the natives were completely justified in their action.

Nothing of real significance took place on the island until 1866, when John Crosby Brown and a group of businessmen from the East Coast bought Pasque from the Tucker family of Dartmouth, Massachusetts. Their purpose was to establish a fishing club to seek out and catch the Striped Bass which were plentiful in the vicinity. The club, eventually established and officially designated as The Pasque Island Club, constructed buildings consisting of a large framed clubhouse, a separate servant's dormitory, and an ice house. Fishing stands were bolted to the shore to ensure that great numbers of bass would be caught during the summer. Chummers, local people who assisted the fishermen, had their own barracks and were even provided a cook to prepare their meals. There was enough room for members to bring along their families and friends. The Club had a long 67 year tenure on the island and only folded because the principle bait became scarce. The Menhadden, a fish of the herring family, is the main diet of bass. Local fishermen from the mainland and Martha's Vineyard were continually catching this fish near Pasque Island for their own use. This so depleted the supply that one summer the club only caught 150 stripers. Finally, the task of operating the Club became too expensive and it dissolved in 1923.

James Crosby Brown, son of the club founder John Crosby Brown then took over complete ownership of the island and until 1928 summered there with his family. Later the Browns used it for occasional visits and eventually sold it to the Forbes family in 1939.

Alexander Crosby Brown, grandson of John Crosby, presently Literary Editor of the *Daily Press* of Newport News, Virginia, later recalled his boyhood experiences on the island in the twenties:

> Our Mecca, Pasque Island, known to countless cruising yachtsmen as a God-forsaken blot of land, is, on the contrary, the most beautiful island in the world. I say this advisedly, having since compared at first hand Tahiti, Samoa, Bali, Maderia, Capri and (lest Sam Morison point out a sin of omission) Mount Desert . . . The critics of Mother Nature's handiwork have not, however, at the age of eight experienced the thrill of "treasure" hunting on restless Cobbley Beach, caught cunners from the beach across the tidal creek, sighted wild deer in a West End swamp, or nightly sneaked out of bed to look for the friendly gleam of Gay Head Light's [on Martha's Vineyard] slow cycle of three white flashes followed by a red. [8]

Mr. Brown's comments show that he, like all who have lived on the Elizabeth Islands for any length of time, became enchanted with their natural beauty.

The next pearl on the string lies between Pasque and Cuttyhunk. One nautical mile across Quick's Hole is Nashawena, sometimes called "Little Naushon."

[8] A. C. Brown, 'Enchanted Voyage,' *The American Neptune*, July, 1947, 213-214.

Chapter Seven

MYSTERY ADORNED WITH FLOWERS

Your pearly bluff,
His Dover Cliff,
Your Merrill's shrine,
His resting place,
Your Sarah's mark,
Her mystery,
Your fragrant bloom,
Their history.

Harold C. Wilson
1973

On a wind-swept hill of Nashawena Island, not too far from where the purple spine-tiped Star Thistle grows, is found a weather-worn gravestone that reads:

Here Lies Ye Body Of Sarah Roon
Ye Wife Of John Roon
Died July 17, 1736
45 Minutes After A 11 A Clock
In Ye 39th Year Of Her Age

Who was Sarah Roon? No one has ever been able to answer that question. There are additional gravesites on the island, but Sarah's obviously was given special attention. It is the only one with an inscription in smooth rock; all of the others are made of crude fieldstone. Whoever Sarah was, why she wasn't buried on the mainland is an interesting puzzle. There is no record of a Roon family ever living on Nashawena. Furthermore, no one of her immediate family has, at any time, been known to visit her grave. One would suspect that she must have been well respected, at least by her husband, because of the time and trouble taken to build her small monument. This puzzling incident is only one of others that mark Nashawena different from the best of the Elizabeths.

Nashawena lies between Pasque and Cuttyhunk. In fact, the Indian meaning for Nashawena is "it lies between." The island is three miles long and one mile wide, about half the size of her sister island, Naushon. She possesses a rather large stunted tree growth at her eastern end near Quick's Hole. However, the rest of the island is treeless, except for some scattered Pine and Oak in many of the small valleys and troughs which characterize the interior.

About two-thirds of the way west from Quick's Hole is Saddleback Hill (on a map the whole island appears to look like a saddle). Just east of this hill is Middle Pond, once called Wash Pond because the multitude of sheep which were raised on the island were given a bath in its waters before shearing time.

The many swampy hollows that dot the island are covered by a dense tangle which makes them impenetrable. In and around these low places 335 of the Elizabeth Island's 558 species of flowering plants and ferns are found. In 1930, John M. Fogg noted that 81½ percent of all plant life on the Elizabeth Islands was native,[9] but some of the flowers found on Nashawena are quite rare for southeastern Massachusetts. For instance, the arrow-shaped leaves of the Buckwheat with its small purplish-white flowers are found hiding behind the many varieties of Sedge. Clusters of the evergreen Crowfoot's bright yellow blossoms grow in the heavier swamps. These plants are poisonous and years ago were swallowed by beggars for the purpose of inducing artificial ulcers to excite the compassion of the public. Wild Orchids, gray, white and green, with a few solitary pink, are hard to find but do grow there. In the swamps, the large Lily, often with orange blossoms, flourishes.

Sheep raising was the main occupation for those that lived on the island in days gone by. In 1930, there were 700 sheep tended by sheep-raisers who lived in an old stone farmhouse on the north side of the island. The farmhouse, built in 1725, is situated on the shores of Nashawena's harbor, a shallow cove adequate for small boats.

Across the island to the south are Nashawena's awesome Bluffs; a two mile stretch of high cliffs facing Vineyard Sound (In 1602, Gosnold called them Dover Cliff). In many places

[9] J. M. Fogg, 'The Flora of the Elizabeth Islands,' *Rhodora - Journal of New England Botanical Club*, XXXII (1930).

they are practically vertical. Their average height is 50 feet, but in one or two points they rise to over 90 feet. It was just off these cliffs, in 1923, during the Prohibition era, that the rum-runner *John Dwight* sank to the bottom of Vineyard Sound.

Early in the morning of 7 April 1923, the Coast Guard at the Gay Head Life Boat Station on Martha's Vineyard were interrupted at breakfast time by several loud blasts from a boat whistle across the Sound. There was a very thick fog that morning and the air was still. After a few moments of complete silence, the Coast Guard then heard an extraordinary number of boat whistles, clanging bells, and what seemed to be men shouting and screaming. The commotion seemed to be coming from the direction of the west end of Nashawena Island. However, because of the heavy fog, the Coast Guard was unable to launch its life boats. They just sat there helpless and listened. After several minutes of this commotion from the sea, a soft quietness again returned. In a few hours, the fog lifted enough so that the Coast Guard could see an unknown vessel pitch and roll and then sink, quickly to the bottom of the Sound. At once, the life boats were launched and converged on the area. An all-day search proved fruitless. No other boats were seen and no evidence indicating a struggle was discovered. It was as if the incident had never happened. Because night was approaching, the puzzled and frustrated sailors returned to their station.

The next day, local fishermen began finding bodies being washed ashore and eventually picked up eight dead men. Sea divers determined the name of the ship; plainly printed on the stern was *John Dwight*. Some of the bodies were badly cut and bruised indicating that they had been involved in a severe struggle. All were well dressed young men, clearly not ordinary seamen. A multitude of air-tight barrels of Canadian Ale were discovered drifting in the nearby waters.

An extensive investigation was not able to determine the identity of the bodies or the owner of the vessel. Today, the case still remains a mystery. But there is a possible solution to the riddle. Shortly before the incident off Nashawena, a "rum running war" was brewing. Local rum-runners were continually being harassed by "rum pirates" from Long Island and points south. Perhaps the men of the *John Dwight* were the leaders of this pirate group. Or, a more logical hypothesis would be that they were members of the "organization", a kind of "Mafia", if you will. Unable to get their share of the profits from the local "runners" by ordinary means, they took matters into their own hands and, as a result, lost their lives because they were unable to cope with the cunning of the "yankee sailors", especially in their own "home grounds". As so often happens today with the narcotics racket, the inevitable confrontation between little guys and big guys resulted in murder. However on 7 April 1923 the little guys came out on top.

Probably the most baffling mystery on Nashawena is the Merrill Monument which stands in the exact center of the Island. Edward Merrill of New Bedford, Captain of a Whaler, retired at the relatively young age of forty. In 1880 he bought Nashawena and spent his remaining years there reading the Bible and Shakespeare. Prior to his death, he instructed the caretaker of the island to erect a twenty-five foot tower in his memory. The monument, he insisted, would have to be located over his grave. Several years after the death of Captain Merrill in 1884, the caretaker, along with a group of men from Cuttyhunk Island, carried out this rather bizarre request.

This stone memorial stands over the body of a man whose only claim to fame was that he was an ordinary sea captain among hundreds of other sea captains in the Cape Cod and New Bedford area. Is it possible that he felt he had contributed something of significance to humanity that we are unaware of? Whatever his secret reasons, Captain Merrill thought it proper to erect his own shrine. My guess is that the Captain had the memorial tower built, not for himself, but for the island he loved. Perhaps his boyhood dream had been to have his own "little island" where he could rule supreme. Old and near death and thankful that this dream had become a reality, he wanted people to know that he was once the sovereign of the most beautiful island on Earth.

The reader might suspect that Nashawena with her enigmatical episodes, is the most mysterious isle of the Elizabeths. But this is not so. Just under one nautical mile to the northwest of her lies Penikese with its serpentine head scowling at man. If Penikese could speak, it would say: "Nashawena, you will never have the secrets I possess!"

Chapter Eight

THE ISLAND OF EVIL

On the isle of Penikese,
Ringed about by sapphire seas,
Fanned by breezes salt and cool,
Stood the Master with his school.
Said the Master to the youth:
"We have come in search of truth,
Trying with uncertain key
Door by door of mystery;
We are reaching through his laws,
To the Garment hem of cause . . ."

John Greenleaf Whittier

Penikese is the only substantial island of the Elizabeth chain that sits off by itself in Buzzards Bay, about a mile due north of Cuttyhunk. It has a special story to tell; one that borders on the fantastic. The Indians called it "the sleeping land out in the water", to indicate that it was of no use to them. Today, it is strictly for the birds.

Owned by the Massachusetts Department of Fisheries and Game, the island is preserved as a sanctuary where those interested in orthinology can explore and note the many species of winged creatures that either permanently or temporarily live there.

In the past, the most predominant bird was the Tern which bred on the western side of the island. Mr. Arthur Hollick, noted geologist, made these comments during his visit there in the late 1800's:

. . . It rises from the shoreline on all sides to a height of 85 feet near the center, and is about as barren and unattractive a pile of gravel and boulders as can well be imagined . . . Certain species of terns breed there in immense numbers, and while wandering over the nesting grounds I saw perhaps a score or more of this seasons young ones hopping and fluttering over the grass and stones, evidently unable to fly. Several were picked up in order to examine them, and in each instance it was found that one or both wings were aborted. The number of these cripples were

42

evidently considerable, as I saw the dead bodies of many others. All, of course must have died of starvation as soon as they were finally deserted by the old ones. At the time of my visit the entire colony was yet there and the frightened cries of the cripples at once attracted all the birds in the vicinity, who formed a vast whirling cloud, hovering close overhead, individuals from the mass every now and then making closer downward swoops and all joining in making a deafening noise. It was a sight alone worth a journey to the island to see. [10]

During my short visit there, a few years ago, I found it almost impossible to walk near the shore of the western part of the island without stepping on eggs. The birds seemed to be very much annoyed by my presence and some of them actually attacked me as I fondled some of their young in my hand. The Seagulls seem to be rather violently taking over the island from the Terns. Scattered here and there were several indications of the struggle — skeletons and decomposed bodies of birds. Today, orthinologists, when visiting the island, especially during the breeding season, must wear special hoods to protect them from constant attack.

Penikese, two-thirds of a mile long and a half-a-mile wide, is seventy-four acres in area. It contains many temporary ponds: three small kettle holes hold water only during a wet season; therefore, during a dry season, they change to swampy areas. The island contains approximately the following flora: two species of moss, eighty-three species of fern and one-hundred-and-thirteen species of flowering plants. There are no large trees of any kind growing on the island. Many times, man has attempted to plant trees, but for some reason they never took hold. In 1923, a survey team did locate some rotted Cedar buried in one of the swamps, indicating that an ancient forest once existed there. The entire island is surrounded by a beach of varying widths. The many rocks and boulders near the shore make it very difficult to land a small boat. On the eastern side, however, there is a small cove which affords decent protection for sailing craft.

On a map, the island resembles some kind of pre-historic serpent and tends to partially explain a statement made by the Boston Herald in 1922, "Penikese has been a name of evil omen."

I discovered in my reading that the island once had an abundance of snakes. However, today, few are found. An explanation for this could be that these reptiles feed not only on

[10] A. Hollick, 'A Reconnaissance of the Elizabeth Islands,' *Annals of the New York Academy of Science*, XIII (1901), 398.

43

worms, frogs and such, but also on birds. When their population exploded and they were a definite threat to the nesting grounds, the adult birds liquidated most of them.

One of the most extraordinary human stories of the last century occurred on Penikese in the summer of 1873. It concerned the famous scientist and teacher, Louis Agassiz, who was called *The Master* by his students. Professor Agassiz, of Swiss origin, was an authority on natural subjects from fish to glaciers. In 1840 he advanced his theory on the Ice Ages, declaring that in past geological time, large ice sheets, 10,000 feet thick, covered most of the northern hemisphere. These ice masses not only deposited gravel, till, rocks, and boulders in many areas of the world, but also carved and re-shaped the landscape.

In 1848, he accepted a professorship of Zoology at Harvard University. In his long career there he became personally devoted to his students; in fact, many of them became co-workers with him on many of his projects. Agassiz discouraged his students from becoming dominated by textbooks, especially in the study of nature. Rather than the traditional book orientated method, he believed in the more "direct approach" of learning. His favorite saying was, "If you study nature in books, when you go out of doors, you cannot find her."

Louis Agassiz' dream was to establish an outdoor school and laboratory on natural history. He made several futile attempts to organize one. To many people, his proposal seemed too radical and impractical as a useful form of education. With rare will and determination, Agassiz finally convinced John Anderson, owner of Penikese and a wealthy New York merchant, to assist in his project. Anderson was so taken by the professor's idea that he gave him the island outright and tossed in $50,000 for good measure, a considerable amount of money for those days. This occurred in the spring of 1873, and the delighted, if not exhuberhant, Agassiz began preparing to open his school that summer. The opening date was set for 8 July 1873. Initially he planned that the school would accommodate 50 students, carefully selected from colleges and universities. However, Agassiz really saw its future as a research center for scholars as well as students.

May and July of 1873 was a busy, if not hectic time, at the island. An old barn was being renovated for use as the lecture hall. Dormitories were hastily being erected. A small schooner,

44

Sprite, was being fitted for use as a research vessel to dredge for marine specimens. Two days before the school was scheduled to open, work was still not completed — far from it. Agassiz saw fit to play a "Vince Lombardi" role, giving his carpenters a pep talk which probably contained this statement, "We are doing this, not for money but for education." The carpenters responded by working furiously for the next two days from dawn to dusk, finishing up the still incomplete buildings by candlelight. The following morning, 8 July 1873, the John Anderson School of Natural History opened its doors to eager students, 35 men and 15 women.

This was the first school of its kind in this country and was the pioneer of all the marine laboratories and zoological stations since founded along our shores. In 1895, one of the pupils of the school, a female, published an account of her experiences. Unfortunately, she did not wish to have her name placed on the book, therefore, it remains anonymous. The following description of the school is based on her recollections.

The long and narrow dormitory was, in the first few weeks, divided into two separate compartments by sailcloth suspended from the ceiling by a cord. The side of the building facing Buzzards Bay was for the ladies and the other side for the men. An early breakfast was prepared by Negro cooks around seven o'clock in the morning. All or part of the student body would then spend the rest of the morning in the old barn hearing lectures. Those not attending lectures would take short field trips, exploring or collecting various specimens. The students would disect various fish and other animals at a drop of a hat. Lunch was served at noon. After lunch, there was a similar routine until tea time at 3 p.m. Occasionally there was a lecture after dark, and some of the students would even try their luck at disecting specimens by candlelight. The school program included:

> Daily lectures by Louis Agassiz on Geology and Natural History.
> Professor Morse's lectures on Shells and Mollusks (shellfish).
> Professor Packard's lectures on Crustaceous Animals and Insects.
> Professor Bicknell's workshops on Microbiology.
> Professor Jordon's lectures on Marine Algae.
> Professor Guzat's lectures on Physical Geography.
> Mr. Brewer's lectures on Ornithology.
> Mr. Hawkin's lectures on Extinct Mammalians.
> Mr. Roetter's workshops on Drawings.

Another dozen teachers were on hand to occupy any spare time the students thought they might have had.

Sunday was a day of rest and relaxation. In the early evening, a community sing was usually held on the highest hill of the island overlooking Buzzards Bay. Sometimes the Negro cooks would join the group and sing the songs peculiar to their culture. The New Bedford Standard Times in 1961 described the school as, "an ideal place for clambakes, classes, lovemaking and learning."

During the summer of 1873 the school was a complete success. Many of the students, and all of the teachers, anxiously awaited for the next year. However, tragedy struck the budding young institution. Louis Agassiz, who had been in poor health for some time, died during the winter. His son, Alexander, took over as director of the school and it performed moderately well again in 1874. But things definitely were not the same without Agassiz. The absence of the personal presence of *The Master* caused the school to languish and eventually to die.

But Louis Agassiz had already made his mark on history. His ideas on learning, exemplified by the Penikese school, have made a great impact on the teaching of science. Today, many teachers in secondary schools across the country and around the world incorporate the "field trip" into their curriculum. The Marine Biological Laboratory and the Oceanographic Institution in Woods Hole, Massachusetts, both giants in the field of marine science, are examples based on the Agassiz technique. *

Agassiz expressed his philosophy of education in these remarks delivered on the opening day of the school at Penikese:

You will find the same elements of instruction all about you wherever you may be teaching. You can take your classes out, and give them the same lessons, and lead them up to the same subjects you are yourself studying here. And this mode of teaching children is so natural, so suggestive, so true. That is the charm of teaching from Nature herself. No one can warp her to suit his own view. She brings us back to absolute truth as often as we wander. [11]

The Louis Agassiz experiment on Penikese lasted only two years but another kind of experiment had a much longer existance

* In 1973, a committee of interested scientists were instrumental in planning a 100 year anniversary celebration in honor of Agassiz and his school. Professor Donald J. Zinn of the University of Rhode Island, Dr. Bostwick Ketchum of the Marine Biological Laboratory, Dr. Charles Innis of the Woods Hole Oceanographic Institution, and Mr. Jeff Allen, who was the honorary chairman, led the committee. This effort was not only a tribute to Agassiz but also to those modern-day followers who showed a deep appreciation of his work.

[11] E. Shay and F. Shay, ed., *Sand In Their Shoes* (Boston: Houghton, Mifflin Co., 1951) 344-345.

on the island: a Leper colony was established by the state of Massachusetts there in 1905. This was the beginning of a wretched sixteen year experience, both for the patients and those who cared for them. In the early 1900's leprosy was still a hideously terrifying disease surrounded by superstitution. The disease, characterized by a thickening of the skin around the face and extremities and many small bumps of a dusky red or dark gray color on the entire body, had been feared by many ever since Biblical times.

In 1904 and early 1905, a few cases of the dreaded disease were reported in the Cape Cod area. Immediately, the general public was aroused. This prompted the Massachusetts Board of Charities (now the Department of Public Welfare) to find a place to confine all those that were suspected of having this disease. However, as might be expected, no one wanted a group of lepers huddled in their backyard. Many towns, for example Brewster on Cape Cod, were approached and refused. Finally, almost in desperation, the state bought Penikese from George and Fred Homers of New Bedford. Within a few days of the purchase of Penikese, twenty human outcasts of society were transported to the serpent-shaped island to spend the rest of their days.

An out-patient and treatment center was located on the east end of the island where Dr. Frank Parker (who succeeded Dr. Louis Edmunds after the first year), his wife, and several aides cared for the basic needs of the lepers. Small crudely built cottages were erected for the derelicts on the extreme west side of the island. These poor sufferers spent many long and lonely hours in their little huts with nothing to do but wait for death. Many sad cases, such as that of Archie Thomas, a teenage leper, have been recorded. When he was brought to Penikese, his grieving mother came with him and literally held his hand and tried to make his life a little more bearable. Inevitably, Archie died of pneumonia. When the lepers died, Dr. Parker had the almost unbearable task of burying them. Their bodies were laid to rest on the far north side of the island, suspended in quicklime. This procedure was used to reassure the Doctor that the highly contagious disease would not spread, even after death.

In 1921, when only six lepers were still alive, the colony disbanded. These six sorrowful looking creatures were then transferred to a hospital in Carrville, Louisiana. In 1924 the island was given to the Massachusetts Division of Fisheries and Game. The birds now have the island to themselves which was probably how it should have been all along.

I often wonder about this island. Is it just a coincidence that man and animals have found it difficult if not impossible to survive there for any length of time? Certainly, the recorded history of Penikese shows that only the birds are able to adapt to this pile of rock, sand, and gravel. One might suspect that there is some kind of curse connected to the island, considering the stories explained in this chapter. However, I believe the island has a certain kind of haunting beauty. In summer, when the terrifying birds are no longer aggressive in the protection of their young, one could not find a more ideal place for picnicking and catching the cool ocean breezes from all points of the compass.

Unlike Penikese, however, Cuttyhunk Island has a permanent population of people who radiate their friendship to visitors. Even the deer on the island are gentle. Sometimes Cuttyhunk is called, "a little bit of heaven."

Chapter Nine

EACH BREEZE IS FROM THE OCEAN

O little isle of Cuttyhunk!
So far from life's commotion
Each golden hour from care is free
Each breeze is from the ocean.
Here peace and quiet can be found
No trace of cities' roar
Here bird and flower greet morning sun,
On dew bathed rolling moor.

Anonymous

Stu, the bridgetender at Woods Hole, once told me about the pirates of Cuttyhunk Island. He claimed that Cuttyhunk men of the early 1900's lured passing vessels onto Sow and Pigs Reef by conveniently moving the beacon lights at the west end of the island. More than a few times, the ships would smash into the rocks and lay stricken. After the ship was abandoned, Cuttyhunkers would swoop down upon it like a swarm of ospreys and take what they wanted.

Of course, there are some skeletons in everyone's closet, but this story was difficult for me to believe. Even if there is only a microscopic grain of truth in Stu's tale, I think this chapter will show that the story of Cuttyhunk and its people is most remarkable. Not only are Cuttyhunkers courageous, but they are also friendly and hospitable.

Cuttyhunk is situated way out in the water, some twenty or so miles southwest of New Bedford, Massachusetts. It is about two-and-a-half miles long and one-half to one mile wide. On a map, it resembles a lobster with its rocky tail, now under water, at the western end. This ledge is called Sow and Pigs Reef.

Cuttyhunk is mostly treeless; and there is no evidence that there has been any forest growth during the last 300 years or more. In 1858, not a decaying stump could be found above ground

49

anywhere. The lack of trees is probably due to the exposed nature of the island, the prevailing southwesterly winds preventing any large tree population from becoming established. The vegetation is mostly of the bush variety, intermingled with several kinds of flowering plants and herbs. The Wild Aster, the Ox-Eyed Daisy, and the Queen Ann's Lace are found here as well as Indian Tobacco and Ground Nuts. The yellow flowered Tansy plant thrives. A ground up mixture of this plant makes an excellent bitters with an alcoholic beverage, such as Gin and Tonic. The rich people of the Cuttyhunk Fishing Club loved Gin and Tansy so they grew their own Tansy garden near the clubhouse to make sure they would not run out. The plant is poisonous to animals and contains a drug, which when taken in large amount by humans can have a hallucinatory effect. Was it possible, I wonder, that members of the Cuttyhunk Club were "hooked" on Tansy? Maybe this was the reason why they disbanded early in the twentieth century.

The Rose Hip bush, with its red and white blossoms later producing bright orange fruit, is found just about everywhere. Other predominant bushes include Bayberry, Sumac, and a scattering of low Scrub Pine. The bushes grow so close together that, from the air, they appear to form a thick carpet of green.

The island is a stop-over for migrating birds. The Orange Crowned Warbler, the Ruby Throated Hummingbird, and the Scarlet Tanager are found here. In winter, the Chicadee and English Sparrow dart here and there through the bush of the island. Seabirds are numerous with terns, and many kinds of gulls. Occasionally, a Fish Hawk is seen circling overhead with its beady eyes trained on a Tinker Mackeral. It is a sight to observe these buzzard like birds dive from a considerable height to capture their prey a few feet below the surface of the water. Along the beach, Purple Sandpipers scurry along pecking for food.

Turtles were once very numerous in the pond at the west end of the island, but the hurricane of 1938 changed this once fresh water lake into an environment for sealife. In one terrific assault by wind and waves, the waters of Buzzards Bay burst through a barrier beach that had separated the pond from the sea. Now, a channel accepts the running tide daily.

The deer is the king of the island bush country. Cuttyhunk deer are numerous and friendly. One morning at sunrise while walking along the path to the west end of the island, I met a buck and five does. To my amazement, I found myself standing within only ten yards of them. For what seemed like several minutes, we just stood there and looked at each other. Curious, I reached to the right and carefully picked some Rose Hips from the bushes beside me. I then offered the deer a fistfull of this fruit by extending my arm. They seemed curious, too, and their ears stood up straight waiting for my next move. I, then, deliberately made a soft step towards them and then another. At once, they leaped into the bush on either side of the narrow five foot wide path and disappeared. I suspect that with a little determination and patience, man could train the deer to accept him as a friend on this island. Some deer pay regular visits to the village on the east end, seeking food and maybe even some human companionship.

During this same walk, I had a rather startling experience at the west end of the island. My objective was to swim across the narrow space of water between the main island and the small isle that contains the Gosnold memorial monument, a distance of about thirty yards. I put on my face mask, fastened the flippers, and inserted the mouthpiece of the snorkle securely. Without haste, I plunged into the chilled water and moved like a baby walrus, slowly cruising on the surface with my eyes focused on the muddy bottom. About half way across the channel, I rested on the top of the water. Unexpectedly and suddenly, a loud thrashing and splashing of water caused me an instant of terror. I reached out with my hand and felt the side of a hairy beast. After swallowing considerable water while swimming away as fast as possible, I looked to see what I had touched. I saw a large buck, also, swimming as fast as he could away from me. Apparently he had mistaken me for a doe and was as shocked and surprised by the encounter as I was. I made it safely to the isle a short distance away and again looked back at the buck. He had reached the other side, and he gave me, what I thought was a disappointed look, and then darted into the bush. If there is a moral to this story, maybe, it is that man should just accept the friendliness of Cuttyhunk deer and not to become too entangled with their habitat.

The life style of Cuttyhunkers, at times, can be compared with that of the deer: quiet, peaceful and friendly. There is a permanent population of about 21 families. Cuttyhunk is the only island of the Elizabeths that maintains a year round group of people. In summer, the numbers increase to around two hundred. The village is situated on the side of a hill facing the harbor. Beside homes it contains a small meeting house, a school, a library, and a store that has a habit of moving from one place to another.

Progress in education on the island has been considerable since the turn of the century. In 1903, there were twenty students and three teachers; a student-teacher ratio of three to one. In 1971, two teachers had the distinct advantage of instructing one student, a significant, if not unique, advance in education.

There has never been a report of religious prejudice on the island simply because there was only one religion there, namely, Methodist.

Years ago, during the summer months, the pastoral duties were performed for the residents by a young student from theological school. Because he was not ordained, and therefore unable to perform the marriage ceremony, young "expectant" brides and grooms were at a disadvantage. They could not name their wedding day but had to wait until the traveling minister made his rather irregularly scheduled rounds of the island. Also, local legend has it that there were no funerals on the island because no one died there. Once a resident jokingly said, "I guess we will have to kill somebody to start our own cemetery."

Today, residents are supplied with necessary provisions by the ferry, *Alert,* which in the winter, makes only two runs from New Bedford every week, in summer, the ferry makes the trip more often. But being dependent on the ferry makes ordering food somewhat difficult, and a family must carefully plan its purchases in advance. Unexpected guests could bring on a shortage of certain items. However, one could borrow a pound of butter or a loaf of bread from his neighbor. Better yet, he may trade a quart of gin for three quarts of milk. Bartering, common practice, is sometimes a necessity on the island.

In winter there is a "backroom" store in one of the homes which provides items such as soup, candy, butter, and eggs. Various departments of the store, and sometimes the store itself, may be re-located, especially when business is slow. For example, one time while I was conversing with the lady proprietor and others around the kitchen table, which was then used as the candy department, a customer came in and asked, "Where's the butter today?" The owner simply pointed to the refrigerator. Sometimes the candy is located in a dark closet. However, most of the items in the store don't wander too far from the kitchen area.

I have found that Cuttyhunkers have a great amount of unselfishness in their character. They often give more than they receive. For instance, on two different occasions, Mr. David Jenkins, the village sheriff, let me use his old Ford truck for transportation to the west end of the island. Mrs. Haskell, the respected former school teacher of the island, once treated me to "rye and crackers", knowing that I needed a lift after one of my frenzied escapades on the Cuttyhunk cliffs. Despite this generosity, Cuttyhunkers believe that each man should work for himself. The means of earning their livelihood indicates this. In former times, besides fishing and lobstering their other occupations included life saving, piloting, and sheep raising. Today, fishing and tourism are their principle pursuits.

In the 1890's lobstering was big business. Over $1,000 a year could be realized by each lobsterman, if he worked hard, and many of them did. A typical Cuttyhunk lobsterman's work day involved: Got up at 2:30 A.M., ate very little but usually washed it down with a pint of gin. He usually started lobstering at about 3:00 or 4:00 A.M., and got in about 2:00 P.M., hungry as a bear. He was often too tired to go home so ate at the dock or his wife came down and fed him. His meal would consist of boiled lobster, beans, potatoes, bread, and broth. He was strong, honest, and always quick witted. In short, he was happy.

Cuttyhunkers, in days gone by, were excellent pilots for Whalers and other vessels entering Buzzards Bay. They showed superb courage and daring in their duties. In 1924, the bark, *Wanderer,* the last whaling ship ever to leave New Bedford met its doom off Cuttyhunk. Near the island, at the very start of her voyage, she could not combat the fierce wind and sea of a Northeast storm and cracked her ribs on Sow and Pigs. Helpless on the rocks, she was at the mercy of the tempest storm. Five Cuttyhunk men in a small thirty foot motor boat managed to defeat the roaring breakers and reach the stricken ship. As it happened, all hands had already reached safety by their own means. However, all five men were awarded gold Congressional Life Saving medals for their heroic attempt.

A 1904 New Bedford newspaper report of the death of Captain Timothy Akin points out the almost unlimited bravery of Cuttyhunk lifesavers:

Captain Timothy Akin
Death of Widely Known Pilot and Life Saver

Captain Timothy Akin, well known as a pilot and a life saver and wrecker, died at his residence on Palmer Street Saturday after a short illness. He was 74 years of age. His was a stirring life, and he passed through many harrowing experiences.

Captain Akin was born in Dartmouth, November 30, 1830, a son of James and Phebe Akin. He remained at home until he was twelve years old, when he shipped as cook on the Schooner *Choctaw*. She was engaged in the rice and cotton trade. He put in two winters on this vessel, and for several years followed coasting, [local shipping trade], beginning as a boy cook and concluding as master. In all his experience as a mariner he never tried his luck as a whaleman. During the sixties, just before the close of the war of the rebellion [Civil War], Captain Akin took up his residence at Norwalk, Ct. and there becoming acquainted with Joseph H. Jennings, who owned the east end of Nashawena, he was prevailed on to take charge of the property. This was in 1867 and this was the beginning of his experience as a wrecker and life saver, and with the exception of a single year on the mainland he remained on the Elizabeth Islands until the *Aquatic* disaster, residing during the better part of the time on Cuttyhunk, where he had bought a house. Captain Akin had been at Nashawena but a year or two when he had a chance to save a crew. The schooner *Joshua White* went ashore on that island in the latter part of the night. Captain Basset and one sailor launched the boat amid the roaring breakers and took a line ashore. It was a fearfully rough passage, and the boat was stove to pieces, but the two men managed to get the line fastened around a big rock on shore. One sailor on board the *White* was more terrified than his companions and he tried to come ashore on the line before the line was fastened to the rock. The result was that the man was drowned. The two men on shore found Captain Akins house, and the captain securing a small skiff went to the shore with them and found the crew of the *White* all huddled together on the vessel's house. The craft was fast breaking up. The skiff was rigged as a life buoy and, waiting for a favorable moment, Captain Akin would give the signal for the men on the vessel to haul the skiff on board, and then it would be hauled back again with one man at a time, until all were saved.

Captain Akin had seen the time when three vessels were piled up in wrecks about the island of Cuttyhunk at one time, notably, 1889, when the schooner *Gardner G. Deering* of Bath, and *Hunter* of St. John N.B. were piled up on Sow & Pigs reef and the schooner *Charles F. Sampson* was sunk at Hens & Chickens, all because Vineyard Sound Lightship had broken away from its moorings.

Brig *Aquatic* was wrecked on the west end of Cuttyhunk Island Feb. 24, 1893, and this wreck brought about the greatest grief to the Islanders,

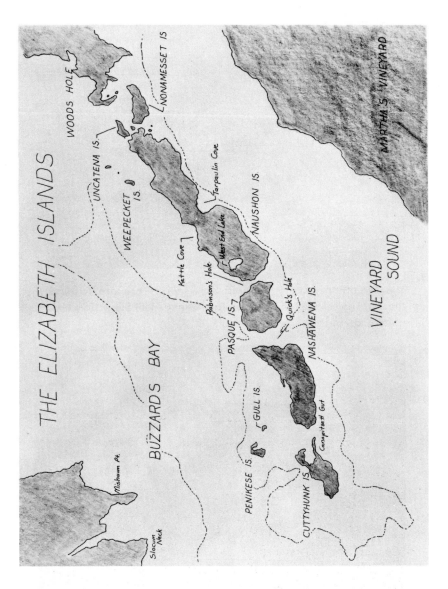

Sketch of the Arthur Hollick chart of 1899. The broken line indicates the former shoreline of the Elizabeth Islands about 5,000 years ago. Then the islands were actually a long peninsula of the mainland.

Courtesy Kevin Kelly

55

The Twentieth century Gosnold Adventurers prepare to land on the Martha's Vineyard coast. The **Queen Bee** alias **Concord** sits quietly at anchor. See Appendix E.

One-hundred pounds of sassafras root is displayed by the twentieth century Gosnold Adventurers at Martha's Vineyard. Left to right are David Clark alias Daniel Tucker, Larry Rogers alias John Angell, Richard Carreiro alias William Golding, P. G. Harris alias Epenow, Jr. and the late Dr. Charles E. Hutchings as Captain Gabriel Archer. "Ruffles" an animal native to the Island sits in front of the group. See Appendix E.

Captain Bartholomew Gosnold standing on Prospect Hill, Martha's Vineyard, overlooking the Elizabeth Islands, 3 June 1602. This likeness of Captain Gosnold is based on the author's available sources. The sketch was done in March of 1973 by Frank Pina, Jr., a student at New Bedford High School, New Bedford, Massachusetts. All attempts to locate an original portrait of the English explorer have, so far, been fruitless.

The northern coastline of Naushon Island. In the foreground is the site of the Pasque Island Fishing Club.

Courtesy Benjamin S. Harrison

Middle Pond on Nashawena Island.

Courtesy Benjamin S. Harrison

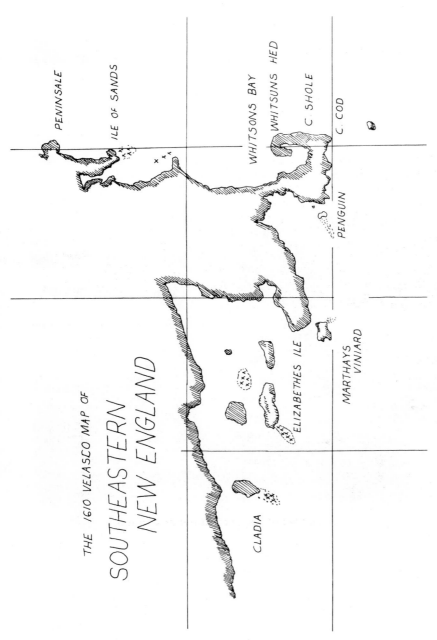

Sketch of a portion of the Velasco map. This map was drawn about 1610 and definitely shows the Elizabeth Islands, Martha's Vineyard and Cape Cod. It is the first known map of the Elizabeth Islands.

Courtesy Kevin Kelly

The friendly deer of Cuttyhunk Island.

The Cuttyhunk Commandos establish a beachhead on the isle containing the Gosnold Memorial Monument at Cuttyhunk Island on April 21, 1974.

Tarpoulin Cove on the south side of Naushon.
Courtesy Benjamin S. Harrison

The backside of the Cap'n Kidd Restaurant in Woods Hole, Massachusetts. On the roof, a local tom-cat enjoys the scenery.

James Crosby Brown, a former owner of Pasque Island. Mr. Brown was Squire of the Island from 1920 until his death in 1930. This picture was taken by his son, Alexander C. Brown.

Courtesy Alexander C. Brown

The John Stettinius photo of the surf off Cobbley Beach, Pasque Island, overlooking Vineyard Sound. The picture was taken about 1895.

Courtesy Alexander C. Brown

The Pasque Island Fishing Club Houses. Picture taken by Alexander C. Brown in July, 1922.

Courtesy Alexander C. Brown

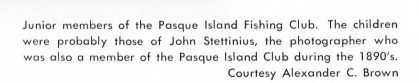

Junior members of the Pasque Island Fishing Club. The children were probably those of John Stettinius, the photographer who was also a member of the Pasque Island Club during the 1890's.

Courtesy Alexander C. Brown

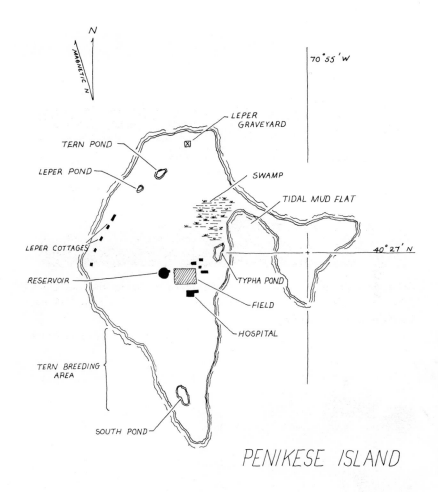

N

MAGNETIC N

70°55′W

LEPER
GRAVEYARD

TERN POND

LEPER POND

SWAMP

TIDAL MUD FLAT

LEPER COTTAGES

40°27′N

RESERVOIR

TYPHA POND

FIELD

HOSPITAL

TERN BREEDING
AREA

SOUTH POND

PENIKESE ISLAND

Sketch of Penikese Island based on a survey conducted by a
group of Harvard University scientists on 24 July 1923.

Courtesy Kevin Kelly

The Agassiz Summer School on Penikese showing the old barn that was used for a lecture hall and laboratory. None of the buildings are standing today.

Courtesy The Vineyard Gazette

One of the largest glacial boulders on the Elizabeth Islands, located near the north side of Penikese Island. The author's daughter, Susan, stands at the base of the rock.

New Bedford High School students exploring the remains of the Leper cottages at the west side of Penikese.

Gary Pires of the Cuttyhunk Commandos drives the **Spirit of Gosnold** sign into the ground with a rock at the site of the Gosnold Memorial Monument. The rest of the group looks on.

Courtesy Michael Labossiere

69

Asa Lombard, Jr. describing the Monument of an Unknown Indian to the Cuttyhunk Commandos of New Bedford High School, Massachusetts.

Courtesy Michael Labossiere

The Monument of an Unknown Indian on Cuttyhunk Island.

Courtesy Michael Labossiere

The Captain Bartholomew Gosnold Memorial Tower at the west
end of Cuttyhunk Island.

Courtesy Kenneth O. Emery

71

cast a deep gloom of sorrow over the settlement and robbed four homes of bread winners.

Captain Akin and wife lost two boys by the wreck, Captain Tim Akin Jr. and Frederick Akin, who, with Isaiah H. Tilton, Hiram Jackson and Eugene Brightman, were drowned while trying to reach the wreck in the life boat of the Massachusetts Humane Society. Only one man, Josiah Tilton, survived the capsizing of the boat, he being pulled on board the brig by the crew the gallant life savers were going to rescue.

Captain Tim Akin Jr. knew no fear, and when he found that there was a wreck and lives were in danger, he gave the word and there were five others just as brave who followed him at his command of, "Shove her off boys," as the life boat reached the edge of the surf. Captain Akin who had heard the news, hurried from his house to the West End of the island and when he found his eldest son was in command of the boat he exclaimed "That boat will never come back; it is a fearful night at the West End." His words proved true. The boat had reached the side of the wrecked brig when she capsized and Joe Tilton was the only one saved. Captain Tim Akin was almost saved three times, but the sea finally drove him from the grasp of the crew who had hold of him by a slender line which finally slipped off his arm. Fred Akin's body drifted ashore the next morning and was the first evidence that the islanders had that the boat had capsized. The same forenoon the stove liveboat came ashore. A day later the body of Tim Akin was washed up by the waves and a week later Isaiah Tilton's body was found.

From that time the lives of both Captain and Mrs. Akin were changed. They could no longer bear to remain within sight of the cruel sea which has swallowed up their sons, and shortly afterward Captain Akin gave up the business which he had followed so long and moved to the city.

Captain Akin was married in 1850 to Pennia Howland of South Dennis. They had 15 children, only two of whom are living, a daughter, the wife of John P. Holmes of this city, and Captain Charles Akin of Milford, Ct.

Captain and Mrs. Akin observed their golden wedding anniversary on July 10th, 1900.

Anyone who has ever been associated with Cuttyhunk people automatically becomes infected, to a certain degree, with their hearty and forthright nature. A good example would be the Islanders' experience with the Cuttyhunk Club which was founded in 1864. This club somewhat like the Pasque Island Club described earlier was comprised of members who had no worries concerning money and was primarily interested in fishing. Besides fishing for bass at their stands on the west end of the island, they generously stocked the then fresh water pond with Black Bass and Perch. In 1880 the club donated land to the Town for a house of worship. On the Fourth of July every year, the members would open their doors to the townsfolk, and they all would have a great time celebrating the holiday. In turn, Cuttyhunkers would assist the members by acting as chummers and gave them expert advice in fishing techniques. Today, the Islanders still cater to the needs of the sportfisherman, all of whom will tell you that Cuttyhunkers are *real* people.

A story of Cuttyhunk would not be complete without mentioning the events and circumstances surrounding the Gosnold Memorial Tower that sits alone on a tiny isle in the Westend Pond. This memorial, made mostly of fieldstone, stands over forty feet high. It is probably the only tower of its kind in the world. One thing is certain. It is no doubt unique in being a tower that can be reached only by a short swim across a pond.

Chapter Ten

A MAN AND HIS MONUMENT

A monument of obscurity,
A symbol for a forgotten man,
A tower that stands alone,
On a spot he did not plant.
A symbol of obscurity,
Misplaced.

Harold C. Wilson

1973

In 1858, historian Daniel Ricketson of New Bedford, swayed by Gosnold's discovery of Cape Cod and the Islands in 1602, proposed Cuttyhunk as the site of a memorial for the first English colony in New England:

> It is truly a consecrated spot and henceforth be devoted to the fostering of that noble and adventurous spirit as well as the kind and friendly relations between mankind manifested in the intercourse of these hardy adventurers with the natives, they here met. In the name, and to the memory of Bartholomew Gosnold, whose bones lie in an unknown grave in Virginia, where he died 22nd August 1607, let it be consecrated . . . A small round and castellated form of tower, built of stone in a rude but substantial manner would be in good keeping with the historical associations of this spot, which might be called Gosnold's tower or fort. [12]

Almost a half century later, Ricketson's fancy language set off a chain of events that finally resulted in the actual building and dedication of the Gosnold Tower. However, the first attempt ran into a snag. Members of the Cuttyhunk Club raised money for the project, but the owners of the small isle in Westend Pond, where the monument was to be built, refused to sell the property. In 1902, three gentlemen, Walter Ricketson, son of the historian, Charles S. Randall of the Cuttyhunk Club, and George Fox Tucker of New Bedford, took the initiative and revitalized the scheme.

[12] D. Ricketson, *History of New Bedford* (New Bedford, 1858) 121-122.

74

These gentlemen managed to secure a promise from the owners of the isle that the deed would be given to them on the condition that after the monument was built, the deed would be handed over to the Old Dartmouth Historical Society and the Tower would be kept as a legitimate historical monument.

With over $3,000 donated by interested citizens, Cuttyhunkers quickly began erecting the tower. On 4 June 1902, all those involved with the enterprise held a small cornerstone ceremony. This date, which corresponds with the old calendar date of 25 May 1602, is the date on which Gosnold supposedly landed on Cuttyhunk. Some of the invited guests who attended were Edwin D. Mead, editor of *New England Magazine,* and George Gregerson Wilkins, president of the Old South Historical Society of Boston. With the following words the cornerstone was set in place:

> We dedicate this islet to Bartholomew Gosnold and his companions, who landed here May 25th, 1602, old style, and built a fort and storehouse, the first English habitation built on this continent. We propose to erect a tower to commemorate that important event, and now lay its cornerstone.
>
> We thus signalize the tercentenary of the first attempt at English settlement on this continent. In this action we take the lead in the long series of Tercentennial celebrations which are to follow. [13]

A little over a year later, the monument, the design of which followed Daniel Ricketson's suggestions of 1858, was completed and on 1 September 1903, one of the most elaborate dedication ceremonies ever held in New England took place on this barren little isle. Three boatloads of dignitaries converged on the isle. Some of the principle participants were Charles Francis Adams of Boston, Henry H. Rogers, Congressman William S. Green, and Frederick S. Allen, the oldest inhabitant of Cuttyhunk Island. Letters from eminent scholars were read, expressing approval of the event. Among these scholars were included Edward Everet Hale, Samuel A. Greene, secretary of the Massachusetts Historical Society, and Paul Revere Frothingham.

Twenty speeches were given, one of which contained this startling statement:

> It [the tower] will stand like the Statue of Liberty, beckoning with a ready finger to Castle Garden and

[13] L. Haskell, *The Story of Cuttyhunk* (New Bedford, Massachusetts: Bradbury-Waring, 1953) 40.

Tammany Hall; and invite imigrants to the cosmopolitan
city of Boston. [14]

Finally, the slate tablet, anchored to the base of the Tower,
and decked by British and American flags, was unveiled. Today
one can just about discern the weather worn inscription which
reads:

Tercentenary Memorial
to
Bartholomew Gosnold
And His Companions, Who Landed Here
June 4 (O. S. May 25) 1602
And Built On This Islet The First English Habitation
On The Coast Of New England
Corner Stone Laid June 4, 1902
Dedicated Sept. 1 (O. S. Aug. 22) 1903
Anniversary of Gosnold's Death At Jamestown, Virginia

The Rev. Leonard W. Bacon closed the ceremony with a
small prayer; and then the large crowd, certain they had performed
a creditable if not significant service for mankind, went home.

However, their well organized, if somewhat too elaborate
ceremonies, crowned with sincerity and enthusiasm did not seem
to influence the general public. Today, very few people notice
the tower and seldom ever visit it. The author considers it a
monument of obscurity, a lost symbol for an almost forgotten man.

I strongly suspect that the monument builders and the others
involved with the project were led astray concerning the correct
site of the settlement which they were commemorating. Historian
Jeremy Belknap blundered in declaring that Cuttyhunk was the
site of the fort, and the monument now stands on the isle with
"egg" on its tablet. Future research will probably show that
Naushon Island, not Cuttyhunk, contains the remains of Gosnold's
activities here in 1602.

But all is not lost. A simple re-wording of the inscription
on the tablet is all that will be required to give the monument a
more accurate historical significance:

In Memory Of
Captain Bartholomew Gosnold, 1571-1607
A Founder of New England And Pioneer In Virginia
His Efforts Helped To Inspire Others To Colonize
Virginia and New England

[14] P. Purrington, "Shakespeare, Gosnold, and the Smoking Rocks," *The Bulletin*
(New Bedford: Old Dartmouth Historical Society, 1959) 3.

76

thus emerged
The United States of America

If this change is carried through, the Old Dartmouth Historical Society, owners of the isle but not the monument, should consider building a small bridge from the isle to span the narrow stretch of water separating it from the main island. This would be an excellent project for ambitious school children of New Bedford and it would also prove beneficial to one particular Cape Cod author if he ever decides to make another swim across this "Isthmus of Gosnold."

Chapter Eleven

THE BEAUTY INFINITE

There is community there,
Overrun with life.
With birds of both sea and land,
Gently screened by wind blown sand.
There is beauty there,
That continues infinite.

Harold C. Wilson
1973

From the swirling edies around the broken rocks off **Nona**-messet to the stiff cliffs, flush with the sea at Cuttyhunk, the story of Those Pearly Isles has been told. Not a complete story, of course, for no history is ever complete.

The preceding pages could be considered as a lesson in preservation — a lesson telling us that certain places must be left strictly to nature as was intended and not to the meddling of man. One would like to believe that Captain Gosnold and his men were persuaded by the Indians to abandon New England's first English settlement on Cuttyhunk (or was it Naushon?) to preserve the islands' esthetic value.

Certainly the line of previous owners must be credited with helping, sometimes inadvertantly, to preserve the islands to the present day. In the middle of the seventeenth century, the May-hews convinced, if that is the proper word, the Indians to live on Naushon. Later, the Winthrops used Naushon as a summer playground. The Bowdoins did likewise, and this tradition was carried on by the Forbes family into the present. All four owners left the island in its natural state. The various owners of Cutty-hunk, Pasque, and Nashawena saw fit to sow seeds and graze cattle on the islands. Nature is again taking over completely on Penikese after the short experiment with lepers at the beginning of this century. Even the British did not molest the islands too badly during the Revolution and the War of 1812.

But what of the future? Penikese seems secure, being a natural wildlife preserve and a haven for birdwatchers. Cuttyhunkers, no doubt, will continue to supply their special kind of hospitality to ambitious swordfishermen and curious sightseers while preserving the peace and beauty of their home. Pasque and Nashawena seem destined to sit there as outdoor laboratories for interested environmentalists.

But what of Naushon, queen of the island group? The Forbes family have kindly offered some of its coves and sandy beaches to boatsmen and their families for pickniking and bathing. However, special permission must be received by anyone who wishes to explore the wooded interior. This, of course, is good and necessary because of the danger of forest fire. Since there is no means to combat forest fires effectively, a large fire could turn the island into a desert by destroying most of the woodland.

Someone once said "Beauty starts when one is born and lasts forever." Certainly that is true of the Elizabeth Islands, and perhaps there should be a monument on Naushon signifying their perpetual charm. Perhaps the best monument would be a simple camp site. I propose that a small plot be selected, possibly on the banks of Westend Pond, on which, during the warm months of July and August, small groups of young people could be allowed to camp for two or three days at a time. I suggest that no buildings of any kind be constructed, that only tents be used. The youngsters, acting as custodians of the island could explore its beautiful growth and present their findings to their teachers in the fall. The place should be called: THE JOHN MURRAY FORBES CAMP SITE FOR YOUNG PEOPLE.

Ralph Waldo Emerson friend of that great naturalist, Henry David Thoreau, once said of John Murray Forbes, founder of the Forbes Dynasty:

> Never was such force, good meaning, good sense, good action, combined with domestic lovely behavior, such modesty and persistent preference for others. Whenever he moved he was the benefactor . . . Yet I said to myself, how little this man suspects, with his sympathy for men and his respect for lettered and scientific people . . .[15]

[15] R. W. Emerson, *Letters and Social Aims* (Cambridge: Riverside Press, 1909) VIII, 101.

Mr. Forbes not only believed in education, but he also had a deep feeling and love for nature. A "Paradise for Children" at the little camp site on the banks of Westend Pond would be a fitting memorial to him. It would also present a solid and final message of preservation for Those Pearly Isles.

Appendix A

THE FIRST REPORT BY A EUROPEAN ON THE ELIZABETH ISLANDS

Warner F. Gookin, the late historian from Martha's Vineyard, had long claimed that Bartholomew Gosnold has been neglected in our history. Gookin has published several articles about Gosnold which have helped to elevate the position of the explorer in history. One fact that hampered Gookin's reappraisal of Gosnold was the lack of anything written by the English explorer. The only thing we have is a short letter to his father, written about seven weeks after the navigator returned to England from his Cape Cod voyage of discovery.

I suspect that future research will, no doubt, uncover more sources to add to Gookin's findings.

In any event, the reader may be able to discern, in the one extant letter, a glimpse of Gosnold's character. The letter shows him to be a man of sound judgement with a great amount of self-reliance. The letter, given in modern English, hopefully does not contain any distortion from the original.

Master Bartholomew Gosnold's Letter to His Father
Touching His First Voyage to Virginia, 1602. *

Anthony Gosnold, Esq.
Grundisburgh Manor
Grundisburgh, Suffolk

Dear Father:

Sorry that I have been unable to see you before this time. I had hoped to leave London sooner, but have been tied up with some important matters.

I received your letter a few weeks ago and understand your dismay concerning my last note that I sent you about my trip. But I thought it would be best to wait and give you a detailed description when I get home (Which I think will be in about a week).

In the meantime, here are a few added lines that might satisfy you about America. We built a small house and fort on a beautiful island that I called Elizabeth's Isle (Do you think she will be pleased?). It is located between two sounds near the latitude of 41 degrees and one third part. I found that the climate is much colder than the same latitude of Spain. Although I do not think it gets as cold as England. I also noted

* Purchas, Vol. IV, Page 1646.

81

that the spring is later by almost a month. Whether this is a normal occurrence or just accidental, I am not certain. An educated guess tells me that it was the former. I'll tell you why when we meet. Furthermore, I think that their summer lasts longer than ours.

I was amazed at the healthfulness of the climate. As I told you before, the inhabitants are tall, well-built, strong, active and, no doubt, live longer than us. All of this is proof, enough. Don't you agree? Verrazzano and other explorers, as is mentioned in Richard Hakluyt's book, show the longevity in age of these people in America.

We were fortunate not to have anyone sick, two days together, during the entire trip. Whereas other Voyagers that went out about the same time we did (especially the Privateers) became sick and some of them even died. Many of them returned long before us.

There is plenty of Sassafras all over Elizabeth's Isle and some nearby islands. We spent most of our time building the fort and house and collecting the roots of this plant which, I understand that a ton of it could cloy the English market.

When I found that we only had provisions for six more weeks rather than six months, I decided to return to England as soon as possible (reason will be explained to you later.) We stayed on Elizabeth's Isle for three weeks.

When we returned and were off Portsmouth, we only had a little vinegar on board and so, were very thankful to see our country again.

I hope this information satisfies you until I can come myself and fill you in on the details which, I hope, will be shortly.

In the meantime, begging your pardon, for which the urgent business of my stay will plead, I humbly take my leave.

Your obedient son,
Bart,

Bartholomew Gosnold, Esq.
Middle Temple
London
7 September 1602

Appendix B

SHAKESPEARE AND THE ELIZABETH ISLANDS

In 1902, Edward Everett Hale, eminent American scholar, stunned an audience of the American Antiquarian Society with his theory about the Elizabeth Islands and Shakespeare. [1] He declared:

Three years ago I was preparing for a lecture on Gosnold, which I delivered before the Lowell Institute. I read again with great interest the four reports of Gosnold's voyage of 1602.

But on this occasion, when I came to the cutting of the sassafras logs by the "Gentlemen Adventurers," I could not but recall a fifth writer of Elizabeth's time who spoke of the cutting of logs (undoubtedly sassafras). I took down my "Tempest" and read the stage directions which represent Ferdinand entering Prospero's cave "bearing a log" . . .

"Ferdinand—I must remove
some thousands of these logs and pile them up . . ."
"Miranda—I would the lighting had
burnt up these logs
If you will sit down
I'll bear your logs the while,
Pray give me that, I'll carry it
to the pile."

. . . This suggestion of a bit of local color in the "Tempest" set me at once re-reading the four narratives with reference to Shakespeare's local knowledge of that voyage of Gosnold's. Any person who gave the account of the Gosnold voyage in brief would say that "here was a small island, heavily wooded, with little brooks of fresh water where the ship could supply itself." He would describe the arrival of the small vessel in one of those coves from which two parties of men go out . . . These parties go to work separately, and the gentlemen cut sassafras logs for the return cargo. They are lost out at night in a storm. They are obliged to feed on the products of the island, which prove to be mussels, from the streams, pignuts dug from the ground and scamels or sea-mews from the rocks. In their description of the island they speak of it as a small island, heavily wooded, with little brooks of fresh water.

Now when you turn to Shakespeare, you find that the vessel arrives at one of the coves of an island after the tempest, from which two parties straggle off into the island, which is small and heavily wooded, with little brooks of fresh water. One of these parties is kept out in the woods in a storm of thunder and lighting, and the food of the island appears to what Calaban says to the sailors when he is trying to persuade them to give him more liquor:

[1] E. E. Hale, *Discussions of The Drama, III, Prospero's Island* (New York: Dramatic Museum of Columbia University, MCMXIX, 1919), 33-41.

"I'll show thee best springs; I'll pluck the berries; with my long nails I'll dig the pig-nuts, show thee a jay's nest, and instruct thee how to snare the nimble marmost. I'll bring thee to clustring filbrits; I'll get thee young sea-mews from the rock."

After detailing several more parallels between Gosnold's Elizabeth's Isle and Shakespeare's island in the *Tempest,* Hale concluded with these words:

In closing this paper I may say personally that my own convictions that Shakespeare worked from close conversation with the people from the *Concord* (Gosnold's ship) is confirmed by the observation that the "Tempest" does not contain one tropical allusion. Here was Shakespeare who must have met Hawkins and Drake and many adventurers, from the Gulf of Mexico and tropical seas. He is describing an island which is in communication with the vast Bermoothes. Yet there is no allusion to an orange, a banana, a yam or a potato, a feather cloak or a palm tree, or a pineapple, or a monkey, or a parrot or anything else which refers to the Gulf of Mexico or to the tropics. Does not this seem as if he meant that the local color of the "Tempest" should be that which was suggested by the gentlemen and the seamen who were talking of Cutty-hunk [Naushon?], its climate and its productions as they told travelers' stories up and down in London? [2]

Hale's theory, of course, is based on circumstantial evidence. Although convincing, Hale's statements did not contain any real proof of personal connection between Gosnold and Shakespeare. The only possible exception would be the Earl of Southampton who was the actor's patron and also an important backer of Gosnold's voyage.

The late George Lymann Kittredge, outstanding American philogist, Harvard University professor and Shakespearean authority, recognized Hale's theory as creditable, but indicated that if it could be found that Gosnold knew Shakespeare then it would be more fully acceptable.

In 1940, historian Marshall Shepard of Martha's Vineyard went a step further than Hale when he offered several striking comparisons between Gosnold's descriptions of the American Indians and the natives of Prospero's island. He refers us to chronicles of Gosnold's voyage written by Gabriel Archer and John Brereton, members of the crew as well as to Gosnold's one surviving letter about the Elizabeth Islands. [3]

[2] Ibid.

[3] M. Shepard, *Our Enchanted Island* (Edgartown, Massachusetts: Dukes County Historical Society, 1940) 13-14.

Archer in reporting Gosnold's arrival in New Bedford says:

> . . . Immediately there presented unto him [Gosnold], men, women and children, who with all courteous kindness entertained him, etc. These are a fair conditioned people.

John Brereton describes the natives in more detail:

> . . . of a perfect constitution of body, active, strong, healthful and very witty . . . of stature much higher than we . . . These people as they are exceeding courteous, gentle of disposition, and well conditioned, exceeding all others that we have seen, so for shape of body, and lovely favor, I think they excell all the people of America.

And Gosnold himself writes:

> The inhabitants . . . being of tall stature, comely proportion, strong, active . . .

Shepard then relates this to what Shakespeare has to say about the natives in the Tempest:

> Stage directions III, 3, 24: Enter several strange shapes, bringing in a blanket; they dance about it with gentle actions of salutations, and inviting the king, etc., to eate, they depart.

> Gonzalo III, 3, 39:
> If in Naples I should report this now, would they believe me?
> If I should say I saw such islands;
> (for certes, these are people of the Island),
> Who though they are of monstrous shape, yet note
> their manners are more gentle, kind, then of
> Our human generation you shall find
> Many, nay almost any.

> Alonza III, 3, 50:
> I cannot too much muse
> Such shapes, such gesture, and such sound expressing
> (Although they want use of the tongue) a kinde
> of excellent dumb discourse.

That similarities between records of Gosnold's adventures in the Elizabeth Islands and Shakespeare's play exist is clear. The simple question of Shakespeare's identity has long intrigued scholars. Perhaps a link between Gosnold and the elusive Shakespeare could be found in the Middle Temple to which Gosnold belonged and probably reported. The Middle Temple, a kind of fraternal club, was an Inn of Court located in London. Its membership included many of the most prominent figures in Elizabethan society. In any case, Shakespeare might be among the luminaries who, at least in spirit, roamed the Elizabeth Islands.

Appendix C

THE CUTTYHUNK COMMANDOS

The Story of an Historical Investigation by New Bedford High School Students to Cuttyhunk Island on April 21, 1974.

We are the Cuttyhunk Commandos. Our mission was to determine whether or not Captain Bartholomew Gosnold and his men actually established the first English settlement on the coast of New England on Cuttyhunk Island in June of 1602. Mr. Wilson, our teacher, was convinced that Cuttyhunk did not contain the site of Gosnold's settlement. In the spring of 1973 he wrote that another island, Naushon, was probably the place where Gosnold and his men built a small fort and trading station. Among other things he said that Gosnold's Elizabeth's Isle where the settlement was supposed to have been built does not fit the description of present-day Cuttyhunk. But Mr. Wilson has quite an imagination and he could be wrong. Therefore during our trip to Cuttyhunk we tried to keep our minds open to the problem.

Although we are not history majors and, at present, are not thinking of becoming history teachers or historians, we hope that this story will demonstrate that kids can, in a sense, re-live historical episodes. We found that one learns much more about history when directly involved with it, and it is a lot of fun.

Our story began near the end of the second semester in January. Most of us were in one of the 24 different Contemporary Health Problem classes taught by Mr. Wilson. One day he showed the classes some slides of his Penikese Island field trip held last spring. Besides other pictures of the Elizabeth Islands we also saw his book *Those Pearly Isles* which he wrote for all of us last summer.

There is no doubt that he loves the Elizabeth Islands. During the last class he distributed sheets of paper and said to sign them, if anyone was interested in going on a field trip to the Islands. He was planning to have three trips in the spring: one to Penikese, one to Martha's Vineyard, and the other to Cuttyhunk. Over 500 kids signed for the various trips. Mr. Wilson told all of his students he would select about a dozen kids for each trip and that they would be notified after the February vacation. He also mentioned he would take into consideration interest, attitude, need and physical condition as some of the criterion in making his final decision.

One morning in March during our Homeroom period the following kids received a written message to report to Mr. Wilson's room (B312) immediately: Gary Pires, Jim Floyd, Susan Lafferty, Larry Rogers, Chris Lobo, Lynn Bland, Peg Lyons, Owen Heleen, Dan Starkie and Mike Labossiere. Upon arrival he informed us that we had been selected as "conditional" candidates for the Cuttyhunk trip. If the mental and physical requirements were completed successfully we would then be genuine members of the expedition. He gave us a written outline and preparation paper and told us to study it. There would be a meeting in a few weeks to discuss the trip in detail. Here are the papers we had to study:

CUTTYHUNK HISTORICAL INVESTIGATION
OUTLINE

Purpose:

To examine the interpretation that Captain Bartholomew Gosnold and his company established the first English settlement in New England on Cuttyhunk Island in June of 1602.

Preparation:

1. Study all documents and published material on the Cuttyhunk interpretation.
2. Study all material related to the Gosnold voyage of 1602.
3. Study all alternative interpretations relating to the Gosnold settlement on Cuttyhunk.
4. Communicate with historians to seek opinions and advice.
5. Physical conditioning program.

Investigation of Cuttyhunk Island:

1. Observations of the land and its products.
2. Observations of the wildlife.
3. Communication with the people.
4. Investigation of the West End Pond area.
   a. Gosnold Monument and Isle.
   b. Beach and vicinity.

Post Investigation Activities:

1. Contribute to a paper showing the results of the investigation including any recommendations for future research.

PREPARATION PAPER

Medical history of each participant.

Physical conditioning program to begin immediately. (The following are goals to be reached before the trip.)

1. 7 minute mile run.
2. Push-ups: 100 (10, rest, 10, rest, etc.)

87

Study the following publications beginning immediately (Please read in sequence).

1. The Story of Cuttyhunk, Haskell.
2. A Reconnaisance of the Elizabeth Islands, Hollick.
3. Those Pearly Isles (Chapters 9 and 10), Wilson.
4. Bartholomew Gosnold, Gookin and Barbour.
5. Archer's Relation.
6. Brereton's Relation.
7. Gosnold's letter.
8. Belknap interpretation 1794.
9. Belknap interpretation 1798.
10. Visit to Elizabeth Island, Gray.
11. Shakespeare, Gosnold and the Smoking Rocks, Purrington.
12. Gosnold's Elizabeth's Isle, Wilson, Carr.
13. Did Gosnold Build Fort On Cuttyhunk?, Standard Times.
14. Gosnold's Fort on Cuttyhunk, Clifford.
15. An Indian Returns To His Land, Standard Times.
16. Maps and Charts of Cuttyhunk.

Special Requirements:

1. All participants will meet at Sargent Field, New Bedford, on April 15th to be tested for the trip.
2. Some participants will be required to write one letter to an authority on the subject for opinions and advice.

In a few weeks we met in Mr. Wilson's room for a short meeting lasting only 10 minutes. Mr. Wilson quickly introduced everyone and then explained the outline and preparation paper in detail. Just before the meeting broke up he startled us with this announcement: "There is a good chance of a transatlantic voyage from Falmouth, England to New Bedford in the summer of 1975 when most of you will be between the junior and senior year. This trip will be an attempt to retrace Captain Bartholomew Gosnold's voyage to America in 1602. All of you, right now, are considered prospects for this voyage. Twelve students will make up the ship's company of about 32 persons."

We listened intently while he was talking, not believing our ears. He cooled us down, a little, however, by stating that a lot of luck will be needed to make the trip a reality. Our teacher then closed the meeting, as he does with every meeting, by uttering the phrase: *"Da Yo Ha Gwenda"*, a good luck saying of his that means *an opening in the woods,* taken from the Wampanoag Indian language.

April came quickly. While we were studying the reading material, Mr. Wilson often reminded us not to let his declaration

88

about Cuttyhunk influence our judgment. Some of the kids wrote letters to authorities asking for opinions. The answers would aid in forming our own conclusions when the time came. Letters were sent to Mrs. Louise T. Haskell and Asa Lombard, Jr., Cuttyhunk historians, Mr. Philip F. Purrington, Curator of the Old Dartmouth Historical Society in New Bedford, Mr. E. Gale Huntington, an authority on many things such as Indians and Whaling, Mr. Henry B. Hough, Editor of the Vineyard Gazette on Martha's Vineyard, Mrs. Raymond Emerson, Elizabeth Islands historian, Mr. Philip L. Barbour of Newtown, Connecticut, outstanding American historian and Professor David B. Quinn of Liverpool, England, one of the World's authorities on early English colonization of America. All of the answers expressed views one way or the other about Gosnold's settlement at Cuttyhunk. It was fun to read the replies and then file them in Mr. Wilson's cabinet for future reference.

On Friday, April 5th, the entire company now known as the Cuttyhunk Commandos met after school in Mr. Wilson's room. After taking our telephone numbers he introduced Dr. Charles Hutchings of the School Department explaining that the doctor would accompany the group to Cuttyhunk. Mr. Eugene Wilusz, a chemistry teacher at the high school would also come along. Mr. Wilson went on to explain that the Cuttyhunk trip probably will be the first of its kind ever attempted by high school students and that the results of our findings would be published in the second edition of his book, *Those Pearly Isles*. He urged everyone to finish their reading assignments and prepare for the physical and mental testing which would be held Monday morning, April 15, during our spring vacation. He ended the meeting with his usual *Da Yo Ha Gwenda*.

The next ten days went by like they didn't even exist. Mr. Wilson and Mr. Wilusz had been getting in shape for the trip since early January. Mr. Wilson recently ran the mile in six-and-one-half minutes! Dr. Hutchings had been ill and was unable to do any running. To compensate, he walked a lot. Most of us figured that the physical part of the test would be a joke so we didn't do much preparing. After all we were young, vibrant teenagers; our leaders were "old men".

The morning of April 15 was warm and clear. As we were walking from the dressing room to the track at Sargent Field we saw Mr. Wilson and Mr. Wilusz racing each other in the half-mile. Mr. Wilson had about a thirty yard lead coming around the far turn with only a quarter of a lap to go. With a great burst of speed, Mr. Wilusz closed the gap and they finished in a dead heat for first place. Everyone noticed with some surprise that they were still standing after the race. After Mr. Wilson recovered (it took about twenty minutes) he called the girls to the starting line for the mile run and they were off. After the first lap, they were floundering all over the track. The boys watched with amusing eyes. At the half-mile mark, Mr. Wilson called a halt to the race realizing the girls had run too fast a pace and were gasping for air. Dr. Hutchings commented that Susan Lafferty who runs like a boy should try out for the girls' track team next year. The boys' race was no contest. Jim Floyd took an early lead and increased it throughout the race. The winning time was six minutes, thirty seconds. Jim definitely has possibilities and should try out for the track team next year.

After the push-up test which everyone completed success-fully we took a long walk to the high school preservation site near the skating rink. It is a wooded piece of land about two acres in size which will soon be used by the science classes as an out-door environmental study project. At the site, we sat down among some glacial boulders. Our leaders then asked questions. Most of them involved the description of Cuttyhunk Island and the purpose of the trip. Then specific duties were given. Mr. Wilson since he was the organizer of the expedition would do nothing at Cuttyhunk but have a good time. Dr. Hutchings and Mr. Wilusz would be the recorders and take copious notes of the happenings. They would also respond to our questions while we were on the island. Mr. Wilson did not want the job because of his bias against Cuttyhunk. Gary Pires would make a judgment if the beach and surrounding waters at the west end of Cuttyhunk was a logical place for Gosnold to land and anchor his ship. Susan Lafferty and Chris Lobo would try to determine if there was enough building materials on the island to use for a fort and settlement. Lynn Bland and Peg Lyons would see if the island contained any evidence of the trees, especially Sassafras, which the Gosnold explorers found on Elizabeth's Isle in 1602. Dan Starkie would try to identify some of the herbs and bushes that Gosnold found there. Susan, Mr. Wilson's daughter who accom-panies him in all his field trips, would have the job of testing the soil to determine if it was "fat and lusty" as in Gosnold's time. Finally Larry Rogers, Owen Heleen and Jim Floyd had the important task of finding out if present-day Cuttyhunk and Gosnold's Elizabeth's Isle were one and the same.

Mr. Wilson then outlined the things we needed to bring with us. As for the clothes on our back, common sense should prevail, keeping the weather in mind. Bright colors should not be worn but rather browns and green so that we would blend with the environment thus making it easier to take pictures of the deer that run free on the island. Each person would need a small notebook and a few stubby pencils. Field glasses, camera and compass were optional. Our leaders would supply the rest of the equipment as rope, oars, rubber raft, plastic disposal bags, etc.

Our ETD (estimate time of departure) for Cuttyhunk was Sunday, April 21 at 8 A.M. The boats would leave from the Coast Guard Auxiliary slips in Fairhaven near the Skipper Restaurant. Before that we would muster in the parking lot next to Radio Station WBSM at 7:30 A.M.

Near the close of the meeting Mr. Wilson reviewed, in general terms, plans for the trip. After landing on the island the group would walk to the village and talk to some of the people. Next, on to Lookout Hill which has a commanding view of the Elizabeth Islands, Martha's Vineyard, and the mainland. Finally we would make the trek to the west end where the monument is located to complete our mission. On the way back to the village we would discuss our conclusions with Dr. Hutchings and Mr. Wilusz.

As the meeting broke up, Mr. Wilson surprised us by not uttering his usual phrase of *Da Yo Ha Gwenda* but instead said: "Remember, it isn't what you say or write, it's what you *do* that counts."

The first thing Mr. Wilson did at the dock Sunday morning was to direct us into the two power boats. He even took the trouble the night before to come up with his pet nicknames for us. In the *Hey Jude* were Mr. Wilson, Mr. Wilusz, Mike "The Mad Russian" Labossiere, Chris "the Mouth" Lobo, Larry "the Thinker" Rogers, "Puffy" Gary Pires, and "Salty" Susan Lafferty. Unfortunately Jim "Flash" Floyd had to stay home at the last minute. Mr. Wilson promised to take him to Penikese Island next month. With Dr. Hutchings in the *Midnight Sun* were "Mean"

Owen Heleen, "Dangerous" Dan Starkie, "Powerful" Peg Lyons, "Lovely" Lynn Bland, and Susan "Manure" Wilson.

At exactly 8:03 A.M. the two fast boats were underway, cruising past the hurricane dike and into Buzzards Bay. The wind was southwest and blowing at about fifteen knots giving us a rather turbulent ride (but mild compared to our return trip). Mr. Emile Morad, Commander of the Fairhaven Coast Guard Auxiliary was captain of the *Midnight Sun*. With him was Mr. Richard St. Pierre. Mr. Robert Souza and Mr. Ernest Ross commanded the *Hey Jude*. These gentlemen, residents of New Bedford, have a great community spirit because they supplied their services without cost. But our spirit, at the moment, was *The Spirit of Gosnold:* discovery, exploration, adventure. So through a "smokey" air and a white-capped sea, we sped towards that "little bit of heaven" way out in the water known as Cuttyhunk Island.

The only kid who had any real boating experience was "Puffy" Pires and even he admitted that the trip over to Cuttyhunk was rather "dirty". The two boats drove through and over the high land swells crisscrossed by angry whitecapped waves. The green-blue water of the Bay constantly reached out with its angry fingers of spray and kept us very wet. To break the seriousness of the moment, Mr. Wilson aboard the *Hey Jude* was involved with a minor incident that produced a great deal of laughter. Mr. Souza passed him a green wine decanter half full of liquid and offered him a drink. The commander of the expedition, without hesitation, snapped off the cork and took a huge swallow. Suddenly his eyes seemed to role back, his cheeks swelled up like baby balloons and we noticed some brown liquid leak out of the sides of his mouth and trickle down his beard. It wasn't wine that his mouth contained but about four ounces of Canadian Whiskey (he has a big mouth). Mr. Wilson made a short attempt to swallow some of it but reluctantly leaned over the side and sprayed the stuff into the water. Later he said jokingly, "Just remember kids, you can't tell the contents of a bottle by its color."

At about 8:45 A.M. we could make out the eastern hills of Cuttyhunk clearly. To the north a short distance away was "the island of evil" as Mr. Wilson calls it. Penikese was uninhabited until last fall but now a group of men are conducting a school for wayward kids there. They have built a small house and generally live close to nature. Mr. Wilson mentioned that he thought the school was a good idea but hoped that it would not interfere with the large number of sea birds that breed on the island in May and June. We agreed.

Ahoy Cuttyhunk! At precisely 8:55 A.M., not bad time considering the nasty water encountered during our short voyage across the Bay, the Cuttyhunk Commandos were standing on the dock and preparing for the exploration of the island. Soon we headed towards the village situated close by on a hillside. On the way, two local residents, Mr. Asa Lombard, Sr. and Mr. Oscar greeted us. Both of them wished us a successful excursion. Mr. Lombard while chatting with Dr. Hutchings hinted that he thought the islands, especially Penikese, should be left to nature. From this we guessed that Cuttyhunkers were serious conservationists.

Mr. Oscar's house which contains the village store is also the place where Mrs. Louise T. Haskell lives. She invited us into her living room where Mr. Wilson introduced us, explaining our mission. Mrs. Haskell is the author of the book called *The Story of Cuttyhunk* which we all had to read as part of our preparation. She was very nice and gave us some encouraging words. She also congratulated Mr. Wilson on his book *Those Pearly Isles* but added, ". . . although I don't agree with your theory about the Gosnold Monument." We listened intently.

After our visit with Mrs. Haskell, we climbed Lookout Hill. At the summit there is a great view. To our east we could see all of Nashawena Island plus some of the coastline of Pasque and Naushon which bends like a bow. Although it was hazy, the Gay Head Cliffs of Martha's Vineyard were visible across the Sound to our south. Of course, Penikese to the north, only a mile away, stood out clearly. Beyond the "island of evil" you could just about make out the distant shore of Dartmouth and Westport. All of Cuttyhunk was below us. For the first time we saw the Gosnold Memorial Monument far in the distance to the west. The tall tower standing on the small isle in the lake seemed to us to be a picture of solitude. A lonely memorial to a forgotten hero. Probably more deer than people visit the monument.

While we were viewing this scene, Larry Rogers and Owen Heleen recorded their observations of the island in their notebooks. They were comparing today's Cuttyhunk with Gosnold's Elizabeth's Isle. The boys asked Dr. Hutchings and Mr. Wilusz a few ques-

93

tions concerning their findings. The most important question concerned the lack of trees on the island. Gosnold said there was a heavy forest on his island. Perhaps Mr. Asa Lombard, Jr. who was very knowledgeable about Cuttyhunk would supply a reasonable answer regarding the missing trees.

In front of Mr. Lombard's home is a small stone monument with a bronze plaque which reads:

In Memoriam
To An
Unknown Indian
A Companion of
Bartholomew Gosnold
In
America's First English
Settlement
1602

Below this plaque is a smaller one which states:

Reinterred Here
September 2, 1972

Mr. Lombard who knows a lot about the Wampanoag Indians and Bartholomew Gosnold spoke to us near the monument. He told how several years ago while excavating for the foundation of a house on the island he discovered the remains of a human being. The pieces of skull and other bones were sent to anthropologists at the University of Arizona for examination. They were determined to be that of an American Indian who lived in the seventeenth century. One interesting discovery was that the teeth were worn down strongly suggesting the person's diet consisted mainly of stone-milled plant products such as corn. After the positive identification of the remains, Mr. Lombard with some descendants of the Wampanoag Indians from Gay Head and Mashpee organized a reburial ceremony. On September 2, 1972 the Monument was dedicated and an unknown Indian returned to his land. On good days, an American flag flies over the monument. Below the flag is a red pennant displaying the word, *Poocutohhunkunnoh,* the Indian name for Cuttyhunk. Beneath the pennant a blue banner with the words *Gosnold - 1602* waves in the breeze. Mr. Lombard believes that the American Indians deserve special recognition because they taught the Pilgrims how to survive in America.

Without their help there would be no Pilgrim story. He hopes the memorial will become a national monument someday.

After the talk we asked him for his opinion concerning the true whereabouts of Captain Gosnold's settlement. He responded by saying that he thought the Gosnold Monument on the west end of the island was in the right place. He reinforced this statement by declaring that although today's Cuttyhunk does not seem to fit the description of Elizabeth's Isle and is much smaller than what Gosnold said it was in 1602, the island used to be connected to nearby Nashawena Island until 1815. The two islands combined would compare favorably to the size of Elizabeth's Isle which was given by Gosnold as ". . . sixteen miles at the least in compass." He further pointed out that Sow and Pigs Reef, the ledge of rocks that extends some two miles out to sea from the western end of the island now mostly underwater was clearly visible in years past and would fit the description of the rocky ledge Gosnold said he encountered when he landed on his Elizabeth's Isle. He also told us that the forest that Gosnold found here with trees such as Sassafras, Beech, and Cedar were destroyed by fire and besides many of them were cut down for lumber. Today Cuttyhunk is mostly treeless especially at the west end.

After thanking Mr. Lombard for his presentation we began our two-and-a-half-mile journey through the bush country to the Gosnold Monument. The time was 10:30 A.M. Mr. Wilson, Owen Heleen and Mike Labossiere advanced ahead of us in an attempt to take pictures of the fifty or so deer that now live on the island. Careful observations of the landscape were taken during the hour long trek. The path winds here and there like a snake. At times it comes very close to the high bluffs on the south side. Midway in our journey we paused at the edge of the cliffs to view the shoreline. The wind had picked up considerably from the southwest making the sea quite turbulent. Huge breakers crashed against the rocky coast producing a mist of spindrift below us. The beach was littered with all sorts of wood, planking and waterlogged pieces of lumber. All of this was a reminder of the numerous shipwrecks that have occurred off this coast in the past.

When we reached the south shore of the lake, Mr. Wilson, Owen and Mike came from nowhere and motioned us to follow them. Almost crawling through some snarled bushes we reached the lake. Before us, was the Gosnold Monument some thirty yards across the water. Brownish in color, it looked much taller than the forty feet Mr. Wilson told us. After treading a short stretch of rocky shore, the group came upon a beautiful little cove with a sandy beach. Being well protected from the wind, it was an ideal spot for our camp. What intrigued us mostly was the seclusion of the place. In the shadow of this almost deserted Monument the Bayberry, Rose and Sumac bushes, thickly inter-wined, displayed their green and yellow buds of early spring. Small birds such as Chickadees and English Sparrows darted around us. Once in a while a male and female Cardinal blazed through the bush. We felt at home in this small spectacle of nature away from the city and classroom.

Our thoughts were quickly broken when Mr. Wilson abruptly shouted: "This is where we are having lunch, let's eat." Everyone brought their own lunch except Mr. Wilson who really wasn't kidding when he said he would do nothing on the trip. He "ripped off" bits of food from his daughter and Chris Lobo. He does the same thing during his second and third lunch duty in the cafeteria at New Bedford High. We made ourselves comfortable on the beach and had a good hour and a half break. This was not for all. During lunch Mr. Wilson directed Larry, Gary and Dan to fetch a rubber raft that was spotted by Dr. Hutchings across the lake. The raft would be needed to transport the com-pany to the monument. While the boys were gone we asked Dr. Hutchings and Mr. Wilusz several questions about the flora and fauna of the place. All agreed there was no evidence of a once large forest on Cuttyhunk. No Sassafras was found. An old water-logged stump was located nearby but it could not be determined whether it was washed ashore or once grew on the island. Gos-nold's Elizabeth's Isle was supposed to contain not only a great supply of Sassafras trees but also Beech, Elm, Maple, Cedar, Oak, and Holly. We did note several stunted Oak and Cherry trees during our hike but nothing else. As for shellfish we observed mus-sels, oysters, clams, and crabs. The explorers of 1602 found the same kind. The birds we saw compared favorably to Gosnold's list with many varieties of sea birds. Dr. Hutchings and Mr. Wilusz jotted down our remarks while the discussion was in pro-gress as Mr. Wilson lazily browsed about the lake's shore in his famous "Naushon" hip boots.

Around 1 P.M. the boys returned with the raft and we began to paddle across to the isle in groups of three. This was accom-

96

plished without any mishap in about thirty minutes. Slightly less than an hour was spent at the site examining the monument, and exploring the surrounding tract of land. The isle as Gosnold noted was about an acre in size. However no trees of any kind were seen although there were several kinds of herbs and bushes. Some of them were mentioned by Gosnold such as tansy and huckleberry. The monument which stands in a clearing on the highest point of the isle is about fifty feet in height. Dr. Hutchings told us the story of how and why it was built (see chapter 10). During our visit no trace of a fort was found. No doubt, anything of value would have disappeared over the last 372 years.

Before leaving a short ceremony was held just to the north of the monument. While everyone looked on, Gary Pires drove a sign into the ground with a large rock. It reads:

The Spirit of Gosnold

Was Here

April 21, 1974

N.B.H.S. Students

After the little observance, we started across Mr. Wilson's "Isthmus of Gosnold". The only accident occurred with the last person leaving the raft on the other side. Chris Lobo because she didn't want to get her feet wet jumped on Mr. Wilson, piggyback style. However she instantly lost her grasp on his shoulders and for a few seconds her head was bobbing in and out of the water like an apple in a tub during a Halloween party.

With most of the mission completed preparations were made for the return journey to the village. On the way our conclusions were discussed with Dr. Hutchings and Mr. Wilusz. Mr. Wilson and Mike Labossiere advanced ahead of us again on a picture taking excursion, seeking out the not too elusive deer. It was a leisurely trip back to the pier where the two boats were already waiting for us. Soon Mr. Wilson and Mike joined us and we climbed aboard. The captains warned the group that the sea conditions had worsened because the southwest wind was blowing around twenty five knots. We better be prepared for a rough ride home. At 3:30 the *Midnight Sun* and *Hey Jude* cruised out of Cuttyhunk harbor. Some of us whispered a fond farewell to that "little bit of heaven." "Prospero's Isle" as Mr. Wilson calls Cuttyhunk was everything that he said it was: Man and Nature co-existing in a very harmonious way.

97

The following hour will be remembered by all of us for a long time. Huge ten foot waves leaping across the bows of the two boats completely drenching everyone aboard. The cold salt water burning our eyes. In the middle of the Bay it really got "hairy" with giant blue-green landswells seemingly moving every which way. Our expert captains negotiated the swells with ease. Like a rollercoaster the boats skimmed along their crests and then plunged down into the troughs. Although there were smiles on our faces, our teeth were shut tight with rigid jaws.

When the boats had reached a point about two miles from the entrance to the New Bedford harbor dike they engaged in a race. Over a now smoother sea the fastest boat of the Fairhaven Coast Guard Auxiliary *Midnight Sun* was upset this time, however, as the *Hey Jude* outdistanced her by plenty at the finish. Those aboard the winning boat gave the captain a three cheer salute. Speeds of forty knots must have been reached during this thrilling experience.

Ahoy Fairhaven. The Cuttyhunk Commandos have returned from their mission, a little tired but content that we had done the job well.

Letter to Mr. Harold C. Wilson Stating Our Conclusions

Cuttyhunk Commandos
New Bedford High School
New Bedford, Massachusetts
April 30, 1974

Mr. Harold C. Wilson
Teacher of Contemporary Health Problems
New Bedford High School
New Bedford, Massachusetts

Dear Mr. Wilson:

You have duped us. We suspect that you really might be the reincarnated Captain Bartholomew Gosnold and purposely took us to Cuttyhunk because you were not sure yourself which island of the Elizabeth Island chain your men built the settlement and fort. Or else your reporters deliberately lied to the General Public for selfish reasons. For example, you were caught in a lie before in trying to persuade your countrymen that the barren little isle of Nomansland was Martha's Vineyard. Anybody in his right mind can easily figure out that explorers would not spend two-and-a-half days on stupid Nomansland finding copper, red and white clay, every bush and tree under the sun, and grape vines so thick that your men could not even penetrate them. Today, present-day Martha's Vineyard still has all of those items whereas Nomansland has nothing. Come on now, does it take a day's sail to get from one end of Nomansland to the other? It is only a mile in length!

Based on our reading assignments and visit to Cuttyhunk we think the island looks the same now as it did in 1797 when historian Jeremy Belknap declared it the place of the settlement. Like Balknap we found no trees such as Sassafras. We saw no evidence of a fort although Belknap discovered a small hole with some rocks lined up around it. But you must admit, Mr. Wilson, things change over the years. Although the lack of Sassafras is damaging evidence against Cuttyhunk it is not conclusive. The soil was pretty good and Mr. Lombard told us that the early settlers "fired" the island of trees for sheep grazing purposes. We did find, however, an isle in a lake. The only one in the Elizabeth Islands that comes close to Gosnold's description. Although the anchorage and beach, nearby, would not be the ones we would select, maybe Gosnold's ship *Concord* used the other side of Cuttyhunk for a haven. This would be the common sense thing to do because it is more protected there.

We conclude, therefore, since there have been so many changes on the island in the last 372 years and since Jeremy Belknap, a historian, declared it the actual place of the settlement that Cuttyhunk is Gosnold's Elizabeth's Isle. Belknap found no artifacts at his choice, Cuttyhunk; and you found none at your choice, Naushon Island. So as in a prize fight between a champion and a contender when there is a draw the champion still retains his title. In this case Cuttyhunk wins. Sorry, Mr. Wilson, this is the way we see it. We agree with Mr. Lombard that the Gosnold Memorial Tower is situated in the right place.

But one thing we are sure you are correct about, Mr. Wilson. The island of Cuttyhunk is beautiful and the people are great. We will never forget this trip. In closing this letter we would like to list a few recommendations for the people of Cuttyhunk that might help to improve their island.

1. That a small boat be available for tourists to visit the monument.
2. That the monument be repaired. The slate tablet with the inscription is very old and should be fixed up.
3. That the isle be converted into a picnic area with tables and benches. Maybe even some small trails could be created.
4. That there be no more building on the island. Cuttyhunk should be preserved for future generations.
5. That a commission be established to see if both the Unknown Indian Memorial and the Gosnold Tower can be recognized as national monuments. In our reading assignments we found that Captain Gosnold treated the Indians with respect and dignity. In turn, the Indians welcomed the English with open arms and even helped them dig Sassafras.
6. Finally, that some kind of field trip information center be established on Cuttyhunk. There could be two kinds of field trips: one on local history and how it relates to United States history; the other on environmental appreciation for those students that wish to explore the flora and fauna of the island. We think that other kids would like the chance to have the same experience as we did.

Sincerely,

The Cuttyhunk Commandos
Gary Pires
Jim Floyd
Susan Lafferty
Larry Rogers
Chris Lobo
Lynn Bland
Owen Heleen
Dan Starkie
Peg Lyons
Mike Labossiere
Susan Wilson

100

Appendix D
A FIELD TRIP FOR LOUIS AGASSIZ*

Since the summers of 1873 and 1874 and until May 1973 as far as is known, no organized expedition of high school or college students ever explored Penikese. There were, however, a few scientists from various colleges who did perform studies there, and bird-watchers have, at times, visited the island.

When Harold C. Wilson of the New Bedford High School faculty was teaching geology to his senior Chem-Physics class, he talked a lot about Penikese. The island contains many minerals and rocks and its landscape shows how the large ice sheets changed the surface of earth some 10,000 years ago.

Mr. Wilson also told his students something of the weird history of the island. He called Penikese: "The Island of Evil." During the breeding season, numerous species of sea-birds struggle for control of the island. The scene is almost incredible — thousands and thousands of birds fighting for a place to nest. The mangled bodies of terns, gulls and ducks, victims, of the struggle, can be found scattered all over the island. The birds have even attacked people. Indeed the place reminds one of the Alfred Hitchcock movie, "The Birds".

Although Mr. Wilson's students had a difficult time believing some of his stories about the island, curiosity finally overcame them, and with their teacher's help, they organized an expedition to Penikese.

Several weeks were spent in preparation. The students studied the flora and fauna that they might find there. In class, work was done on mineral identification, topography and contour maps. Transportation to the island was provided by Mr. Benjamin Baker of the Coast Guard Reserve; and on Sunday, May 20, 1973 at exactly 8:35 in the morning, the group boarded Mr. Emile Morad's power boat, *Midnight Sun* and left Fairhaven, bound for Penikese.

The exploring party consisted of six New Bedford High School students, four adults, and Mr. Wilson's 12 year old daughter, Susan. They were: Harold C. Wilson, Eugene Wilusz, Dr. Charles Hutchings, Robert Maucione, Richard Fournier, Paulette Jadlowic, Gordon Santos, Frank Rodrigues, James Whitehead, Carol Periera and Susan. With a calm sea and little wind, *Midnight Sun* plowed

* Courtesy Dukes County Historical Society.

across the blue-gray waters of Buzzards Bay towards Penikese, some fourteen miles away. The fast power boat reached the island at about 9 o'clock. Penikese is not an easy place to land. However, Mr. Morad is an experienced boatman. He is the commander of the Fairhaven Coast Guard Auxiliary, one of the oldest flotillas on the coast, and *Midnight Sun* cautiously entered the cove on the east side of the island and then touched shore near an old stone pier. James Whitehead was the first member of the group to set foot on Penikese. The time was about 9:30. After everyone was safely ashore, Mr. Morad said that he would return and pick up the party about three o'clock in the afternoon.

While the landing operation was taking place, thousands of seagulls standing near their nests, were watching the invaders. The green east slope of the island was literally covered with the gray-white forms of the birds. They obviously resented this unexpected intrusion of their nesting ground. After the party of explorers had selected a campsite on the beach, it was decided to stay, more or less, in one group while exploring the island. The plan was to circle the entire 73 acres of the island before lunch. Then, after eating, the site of the Agassiz school would be examined. Before leaving, the party woud spend at least an hour discussing their experiences.

As the group prepared to climb the steep east slope, thousands of screaming gulls took flight and circled overhead. This harassment by the gulls was to be continuous throughout the day. On occasion, the birds would make threatening passes at the group. Mr. Maucione was almost pecked a few times. The great black-backed gulls were the ones most often attacking the adventurers. Gull nests usually containing three eggs, were found on the ground everywhere. One had to keep looking downward in order not to step on them. At the very beginning of the journey, James Whitehead and Dr. Hutchings found a small growth of poison ivy. This was the first time that this plant was reported as growing on the island.

Near the highest point of the island is a weather-worn boulder bearing a bronze tablet that reads,

In Commemoration
Of The
Anderson School Of Natural History
Established Fifty Years Ago On The
Island Of Penikese By
Jean Louis Rudolfe Agassiz
Born 1807 — 1873
The Marine Biological Laboratory
The Direct Descendant Of The
Penikese School Erects This Tablet
1923

Standing near this spot, one could understand why Agassiz and his students were so involved with their work. Penikese contains hundreds of erratic glacial boulders of various sizes. One of them is about the size of a small house, standing at least fifteen feet in height. These rocks contain shining minerals such as rose quartz and garnet. On the outside, however, they are rather homely, being of a brown and gray color, because of lichen growth and constant exposure to the elements.

The gulls have taken over the entire island. At one time the terns had control but only one of these smaller birds was spotted during the expedition. Some Canada geese and a few ducks and their nests were found on the northeast side. Although Penikese appears to be nothing more than a pile of rocks and stones, interesting plants do grow on the island. Wild carrot, rose hip and several types of fern were found, mostly at the eastern end. Seaweeds such as kelp, knotted wrack and fucus thrive along the shore.

As for mammals, the island now has a large population of white-tail rabbits. A few of their badly mangled bodies were found on the ground, apparently victims of the birds. One muskrat was seen near the northwest side. Although no clams of any kind were found, it is supposed that the cove contains a large number of quahogs. The blue-black mussel was found in abundance, clinging to the rocks below the high water mark.

There are four small ponds or kettle holes on the island. At the time of the visit, they were filled to the brim with fresh water. The entire island with its knobby hills and trench-like valleys is a perfect example of morainal terrain resulting from the last ice age,

103

an ideal outdoor laboratory for the study of natural phenomena in general.

On the west side of the island are the remains of the leper cottages, small foundations of fieldstone covered with debris and beach grass. On the wind-swept north end is the burying ground of the lepers. Only eight markers are still to be seen. It is known that sixteen lepers died while the colony was in existence and it is supposed that some of the markers have been stolen. One grave appeared to have been robbed, for there was a rather large hole or depression next to the marker. In the hole was a herring gull nest with three eggs.

At about 11:15 a.m. the entire group gathered at the campsite for lunch. Over an hour was spent relaxing and talking about the findings. Everyone was tired from climbing the rough terrain. In fact, Gordon Santos was exhausted and fell fast asleep.

After lunch some of the group investigated what remained of the Agassiz School while the others continued to collect various specimens. Only the foundation stones of the school remain and it was difficult to ascertain which building was which. Mr. Wilusz managed to uncover a small porcelain object which seemed to be part of a lamp. At around 2 p.m. everyone mustered at the campsite for a general discussion and critique. Notes were compared and Mr. Wilson collected all of the specimens. They would be identified at school the following week.

At three o'clock the *Midnight Sun* arrived and the tired explorers climbed aboard. They left behind a reminder of their visit. A weather-worn log, standing erect at the campsite, bears the following inscription:

Campsite of
Natural Science Field Trip
held
May 20, 1973
by
New Bedford High School Students
for
Lou Agassiz

Perhaps these students felt that Penikese Island was not so "evil," after all, but a place of nature for man to appreciate and ponder.

LIST OF SPECIMENS COLLECTED AND OBSERVED
AT PENIKESE ISLAND
May 20, 1973

SEAWEED

Kelp   Laninaria
Fucus   Knotted wrack
Codium

SHELLFISH

Blue-black mussel   Periwinkle

BIRDS

Herring gull, the most prevalent   Great black-backed gull
Ring billed gull   Common tern, only one noted
Lesser black-backed gull   Laughing gull
Canada geese   Marsh hawk, only one noted
Ring necked duck   Black duck
Blue jay   English sparrow
Red-winged blackbird   Baltimore oriole

ANIMALS (General)

King snake   Common white-tail rabbit
Muskrat

PLANTS (General)

Pig weed   Milk weed
Poison ivy, the first known report of its growth on Penikese
Dandelion   Beach grass (various)
Rose-hip   Fern (various)
Donkey weed   Sedge
Wild Carrot   Iris, found in clumps, central portion

MINERALS AND ROCKS

Syenite   Gabbro
Milky quartz   Feldspar
Smoky quartz   Biotite
Plagioclase

Appendix E

THE REDISCOVERY OF MARTHA'S VINEYARD*
INTRODUCTION

Several worthwhile projects will be presented during the celebration of the 200th anniversary of the United States of America. My contribution to the Bicentennial concerns the re-living of history. In June of 1974 a band of teachers and students from New Bedford High School landed on the rocky shores of Chilmark and attempted to duplicate Captain Bartholomew Gosnold's discovery of Martha's Vineyard in the year 1602. During this rediscovery of the island, these modern-day adventurers assumed the roles of Gosnold's men and for two days performed many of the actual activities of the original discoverers.

My project should not be confused with those re-staged historical events that are conducted by grown men. I once saw such a group, dressed in colonial attire, stumble through "The Battle of Lexington and Concord." This kind of reenactment can prove more dangerous than educational. For example, in 1907 Mr. J. K. P. Purdham of Woods Hole playing the role of Captain Gosnold, lost his balance on a slippery rock while landing on the beach. He almost broke his neck.

My kind of historical reenactment extends the physical and mental capacity of the participant to the extent that he can begin to appreciate the lesson of history. In rediscovering the Vineyard, my students had the opportunity to observe what is left of the island as Gosnold saw it. Today, much of it has become the victim of tourism. As was the case when the white man took from the Indians, and land is slipping away again. By becoming spiritually involved in the rediscovery of the island, my students learned to value not only the Vineyard *left* but also the Vineyard *lost*.

The following account includes the activities performed on May 31st, June 1 and 2, 1974. Since history usually is not recorded correctly the first time, I have taken the liberty to also include episodes accomplished in September and December of the same year. Comments from the original Gosnold Relations are indented. These passages demonstrate some of the remarkable similarities between the two expeditions. Editorial comments are enclosed in parentheses.

Harold C. Wilson

* Courtesy Dukes County Historical Society, Inc.

I have been requested by a dear friend to put down in the writing the account of our recent discoveries in an unknown country. On Friday, May 31, 1974 at 3 o'clock in the afternoon we did sail from Fairhaven in *The Queen Bee* alias *Concord*. The company was as follows: Harold C. Wilson alias Captain Bartholomew Gosnold, Rudolph Matland alias Captain Bartholomew Gilbert, Dr. Charles Hutchings alias Gabriel Archer, Emile Morad alias Captain Martin Pring, John Strittmatter alias Robert Meriton, biologist, Richard Carreiro alias William Golding, goldsmith, Larry Rogers alias John Angell, Richard Harriman alias John Brereton, Owen Heleen alias George Hill, David Clark alias Daniel Tucker, Susan Lafferty alias Robert Salterne, Rene Boucher alias Anthony Gosnold, Karen Durant alias William Strete, Robert Bedard alias Thomas Field, Susan Wilson alias William Johnson, Joanna Wilson alias Richard Belfield, Joy Arruda alias John Martin, and Frank Pina alias John White, artist.

Late that day we saw the coast of the supposed island lying in 41 degrees latitude. Our ship approached the shore and anchored near a great rock which we called The Rock Of Hope. The entire company went ashore except for Captain Gilbert and eight sailors. We were immediately met by the Lord Commander of the country, Mr. Sydney Harris alias Epenow. With him was his son Preston alias Epenow, Jr. Both of them were very kind and courteous and promised to help us during our stay.

This place is most beautiful and the coast very bold. Here we saw sea birds breeding and building their nests. Giant boulders were everywhere. Millions of mineral stones sparkled in the late afternoon sun.

> Here we had cranes, stearns, shoulders, geese, and divers other birds which there at that time upon the cliffs being sandy with some rocky stones, did breed and had young . . . This island as well as all the rest of these islands, are full of stones fit for building; the sea sides are covered with stones, and many of them glittering and shining like mineral stones . . .

Epenow showed us a secluded spot near the crest of a high cliff. Small oak trees provided excellent cover. We established our settlement and trading station there. Hastily we set our fires and prepared supper from our meager supplies. The dinner consisted of bacaluere and mustard (beans and hot dogs). Before sunset

107

most of the company walked to a nearby bluff where the *Sign of Discovery* was placed. It read:

Wherever you or I chance to live, or wherever an Ancestor made his home, it is always the Discoverer or First Settler of that place who is held in special regard.

Such a person is a true Pioneer, one whom we may respect for his hardihood, his will to overcome danger, and his perseverance in carrying into effect those plans and purposes which give birth to every town and nation.

In the business of discovering the New World and settling Virginia, Captain Bartholomew Gosnold was an outstanding Pioneer, and as such, his Expedition to these shores in 1602 is ever of interest . . .

In death he was honored as justly his due, and as we value his labors, we honor him too. (Marshall Shepard)

This Inscription Was Put Here On May 31st, 1974 By New Bedford High School Students While Simulating The Discovery Of Martha's Vineyard By Bartholomew Gosnold And His Company In 1602.

During the time the sign was being placed on the bluff, Epenow and his son looked on with faint smiles on their faces. While walking back to the settlement Epenow bid us farewell saying he would return the next morning and guide the adventurers in their exploration of the interior. Before retiring, some of the company made hot tea from the roots of dandelions to cure their heartburn caused by over indulgence at supper. John Brereton especially had a severe stomachache.

This land is an island said to be almost twenty miles in length and some 10 miles in width. It possesses a wealth of commodities including valuable mineral stones such as garnet, several species of medicinal plants grow here, as skunk cabbage for respiratory ailments, and Indian Pipe, the juice of which cured me of sore eyes during our visit. There is an abundance of fresh water fish in the several ponds and brooks. Salt water fish such as striped bass, and cod are found near the shore but are not as plentiful as before. Deer live in the heavily wooded areas. Livestock graze in the meadows over parts of the island. People from the mainland visit here during the warm months to enjoy its enchanting atmosphere.

Epenow said that the island becomes very crowded in the summer. This could prove to be a serious problem in the near future. The northern part of the island is mostly hilly with patches of woodland here and there. The southern part is a great plain containing several large farms. A beach stretches for miles protecting the fertile marshes which contain several kinds of shellfish (but again not as much as before). This entire island is still a scene of beauty despite the ever increasing influence of the nearby mainland.

> . . . where coming ashore, we stood like men ravished at the beauty and delicacie of this sweet soil; for besides divers clear lakes of fresh water, meadows very large and full of green grass; even the woody places do grow so distinct and apart one tree from another, upon green grassie ground, somewhat higher than the plains, as if nature would show herself above her power artificial.

The next morning it was raining when I, Bartholomew Gosnold, set out with Epenow and his son to explore the country. With me were John Brereton, Robert Meriton, biologist, George Golding, goldsmith, and divers other gentlemen. Gabriel Archer and a few men stayed at the settlement. I told them we would return early that afternoon.

Not far from the settlement Epenow showed us some graves of the early inhabitants. He told us that the bodies always were placed in the ground facing the rising sun. We then entered an area of numerous grapevines which did not yet have many blossoms. At a very rapid pace, Epenow led us through some thick woods of beech, black and white oak, hickory, cedar, and holly trees. The land was somewhat hilly with several large rocks scattered about which might be used for building. Turning eastward we adventurers came upon a scattered grove of sassafras trees. A few of them were over forty feet high. Epenow mentioned that the bark of the root of this tree was made into a strong tea and was a valuable commodity in Europe 300 years ago. Then, it was supposed to be a cure for syphilis. As no one in our party was infected with such disease, I suspect a few sips of sassafras brew might relieve the tiredness which we were all feeling at this point.

The expedition continued the journey southerly and soon turned more to the west. We entered a great plain with scattered oak and beetlebung trees. Most of the tress were covered with grapevines extending some thirty feet above us. In a few places these vines were growing so close together that it was almost impossible to tread through them. I was so impressed with this scene that I called the place Martha's Vineyard.

> . . . an incredible store of vines, as well in the woodie part of the island, where they run upon every tree, as on the outward parts, that we could not go for treading upon them . . .

Epenow, Jr. told us that in October one could smell the fragrant aroma of the grapes from his village one mile distant.

Farther on we came upon large pastures. A small herd of cattle came towards us at almost a gallop but then passed by at a slower pace. William Strete thought one of the animals was a bull but we soon discovered that it was a large black pregnant cow. We called this place Strete's Funny Farm.

At the Indian village Epenow's people greeted us. They were all kind and courteous. They gave us gifts such as buttercup root for our cuts and bruises, sunflower root for blisters, and a special mixture from the bark of a wild cherry tree to cure William Strete's cold. We, in turn, presented Epenow's squaw with divers gifts such as books, scrimshaw, and an old conch shell.

> . . . there presented unto him (Gosnold) men, women and childen, who with all courteous kindness entertained him, giving him certain skins of wild beasts, which may be rich furs, tobacco, turtles, hemp, artificial strings, colored chains, and such like things as at the instant they had about them. These are a fair conditioned people . . .

After a short stay we crossed a trail that we called Cagney's Byway (North Road). Soon the explorers entered a forest of beech, holly, and cedar trees. Here we found an incredible variety of berry bushes as strawberry, dangleberry, raspberry, gooseberry, elderberry, and blueberry. The root of the blueberry, steeped, cured John Brereton of a severe case of diarrhea.

While walking through this elegant wood, a great swarm of yellow jackets attacked the company scattering the gentlemen in panic. John White, artist, flung his sketch pad and crayons in fear when he was stung in the buttocks. Also stung were Robert Salterne, John Martin, and John Brereton in the vicinity of the mouth.

110

After this horrid experience the company crossed a small trail called by us The Lost Road (Taber House Road). There, Epenow showed the explorers a place where ground nuts could be found. These small tubular plants are similar to potatoes and are very delicious.

> . . . Also, in every island, and almost in every part of every island, are a great store of groundnuts, forty together on a string, some of them as big as hens' eggs; they grow not two inches under ground; the which nuts we found to be as good as potatoes . . .

A few miles farther the explorers passed through a heavy forest of sassafras. This important discovery was noted by Robert Meriton, biologist. The next day the Indians would help us dig the root of this once valuable plant.

> . . . The sassafras which we brought we had upon the islands, that a ton was sufficient to cloy England . . . a tree of high price and profit . . .

At last we reached the summit of a great hill (Peaked Hill) where we rested and drank our remaining water. From here one could view much of the southern part of the island's coast and to the southeast a thin outline of another island (Nantucket) which we overlooked in our voyage. Upon leaving we named the peak of this hill P. G.'s (Mishap). Descending its slope we trudged our way through two miles of thick growth, especially thorny bullbrier. Epenow said that the highest hill on the island, Prospect Hill, was due north. I was anxious to reach its summit and observe any new discoveries which might include other islands and the supposed mainland.

During this time of discovery the company had a difficult time trying to keep up with the fast pace of Epenow who was smashing dead branches before him as he almost ran ahead of us. John Brereton and John Angell lagged behind the rest and, I think, ate some food which they had hidden in their breeches. We rested for a short time on a plain at the base of the highest hill. This place was called the Desert by Epenow. The Sachem explained that it was the site of the principal village of past generations of his people. By scratching the surface of the bare ground there, one could still find tools and arrowheads.

111

When we reached the summit of the hill the majesty of our discoveries was realized. To our north there was a large expanse of sparkling water (Vineyard Sound). About six miles across the sound was a string of five islands stretching east to west from the supposed mainland. They formed a boundary between the sound and a greater bay (Buzzards Bay) beyond. The shore of the islands sparkled so that I called them Those Pearly Isles. Beyond the islands we saw the vivid outline of the mainland some twenty miles distant. This land seemed to curve west to east forming the bay.

> . . . at length we were amongst many fair islands, all lying within a league or two one of another . . . and then we came into a fair sound . . . this we called Gosnold's Hope; the north bank thereof is the main, which stretcheth east and west . . . and bendeth like a bow . . .

To the west we saw gigantic cliffs (Gay Head Cliffs) of red and white clay. Epenow told us that we would shortly see smaller cliffs near the shore also containing great amounts of clay. At one time, near the clay cliffs there was a large brick works. Looking southerly, a small isle (Nomansland) was distant a few miles away from us. Epenow mentioned that this island is controlled by the navy of the mainland and also people who are interested in preservation. The navy uses it as a target range for bombing and at the same time, the conservation people try to preserve it. A strange association, indeed. Behind us to the south the wooded rolling hills of this part of the island were in sharp contrast to the rather heavy concentration of people that live in the eastern part.

I had a dream while gazing here: a dream of preservation. I saw Those Pearly Isles and this beautiful island being nourished by the blood of the earth that surrounds them. The blood of salt water mixing with the leaching red clay of the cliffs producing a solution of concord. Sea birds should be allowed to nest on their rocky shore; animals to run free in the meadows and forest; above all, future explorers should have the opportunity to see this beauty infinite around me. Upon leaving this hill, I called it Harris' Hap, in admiration of the Sydney Harris family who use this land well.

The way to the island's northern shore was downhill. Several of the explorers, tired and thirsty, struggled along. Being late in the afternoon, we were anxious to return to our trading station

112

and foolishly sped through a large meadow of bayberry and sumac hiding a great amount of poison ivy. Some of the adventurers later sustained extensive rashes, notably, William Strete, our sailing master, who suffered a heavy eruption on the buttocks.

Just before the explorers reached the northern coast they entered a long and narrow valley. It reminded me of the lush and green landscape of Scotland. I called it the Valley of No Return. When leaving, however, we had to rename it the Valley of Ticks. Many of the company had to spend several minutes removing these blood sucking insects from their clothing and body. William Golding had an especially difficult time attempting to remove some ticks from his mustache.

The spectacle of the island's northern shore was a scene of preservation personified. As the explorers tramped over rocks and boulders at the seaside they saw a huge pile of carbon at the base of a high cliff: this graying black mixture contained evidence of life of millions of years ago. Surrounded by huge deposits of red, white and gray clay, the adventurers drank of the fresh water springs that were found in many places on the shore only a few feet from salt water. Moving easterly the company passed the remains of the old brick works mentioned earlier by Epenow. Fortunately man did not take all of the clay which still is abundant.

> . . . also many springs of excellent sweet water . . . the necks
> of their [Indians] pipes are made of clay hard dried, whereof
> in the island is great store both red and white . . .

The adventurers crossed a fast running brook called by me Tiny Little Stream. (Roaring Brook) It is somewhat polluted now, for it begins at the old town dump of a nearby village but small brook trout still struggle to survive in it. Shortly we reached the Rock of Hope and climbed the face of the bluff to our trading station. What we had witnessed along this coast was bold beauty flawed, by the garbage and refuse of man washed ashore by the incoming tide.

As we entered the settlement, Gabriel Archer and some gentlemen were huddled around the fire. Apprehensive and hungry they had expected us to return much earlier. While we were gone they had had to dig for groundnuts near the trading station and had dug for mussels along the shore.

> . . . yet the want of our Captain [Gosnold] that promised to
> return, as aforesaid, struck us with a dumpish terror . . . in
> the mean we sustained ourselves with alexander and sorrel,
> pottage, groundnuts, and tobacco which gave nature a reason-
> able content. We heard, at last, our Captain to "lewre" unto
> us, which made much music as sweeter never came unto poor
> men.

Epenow bid the explorers farewell and said that he would return
that night with his family. Soon the adventurers began preparing
for the evening meal and the visit of Epenow and his company.

The night of June 1 and the following morning will long be
remembered by all. Epenow came with his men, women and
children and brought with him some cantelope and fresh water
from his private springs. With good cheer everyone sat around the
fire and ate groundnuts, brook trout, crabmeat, and a very sweet
beverage called "coke." The feast lasted for several hours. (It
reminded me of Thanksgiving.) The natives left around midnight
saying they would be back the next morning to help us dig sassafras
and collect other valuable products of the island.

> . . . they sat with us and did eat of our bacaleure and mustard,
> drank of our beer . . . they fell afresh to roasting of crabs, red
> herrings which were exceeding great, groundnuts as before.
> Our dinner ended, the seignior first took leave and departed,
> next all the rest saving four that stayed and went into the
> wood to help us dig sassafras . . .

Early the next day the explorers prepared to leave the island.
Some of the gentlemen and Indians led by Daniel Tucker found
the sassafras and dug over 100 pounds of the root. William
Golding and his men returned to the settlement with many minerals
and about 80 pounds of gray, white, and red clay. Robert Meriton
followed Epenow who showed him a variety of edible and
medicinal wild plants. Meriton collected some of them to show his
countrymen back in England (New Bedford).

At noon the explorers went aboard *Concord*. Epenow with his
son and squaw stood on a high cliff near the *Sign of Discovery* and
waved a farewell. With a sad feeling because we were sorry to

leave this island we shouted *Da Yo Ha Gwenda* (a Wampanoag phrase meaning an opening in the woods). We then sailed northwest to an island later to be called Elizabeth's Isle.

Sol Oriens Spei,
Harold C. Wilson
alias Captain Bartholomew Gosnold

SELECTED BIBLIOGRAPHY
PRIMARY PRINTED SOURCES

Arber, Edward, ed. *The Travels and Works of Captain John Smith*, 2 vols., Edinburgh, 1910.

Archer, Gabriel. *The Relation of Captaine Gosnols Voyage to the North part of Virginia*, Samuel Purchas, ed., Purchas His Pilgrims, London, 1625.

Brereton, John. *A Brief and true Relation of the discoverie of the north part of Virginia* . . . , London, 1602.

Gorges, Sir Ferdinando. *A Description of New England from America painted to Life*, London, 1658.

Hakluyt, Richard. *'Discourse of Western Planting* [1584]', Charles, Deane, ed., Maine Historical Society, Cambridge Press of John Wilson and Son, 1877.

Ive, Paul. *Practise of Fortification*, Thomas Orwin, London, 1589.

Manningham, John. *Diary of John Manningham of the Middle Temple*, Camden, Society, 1868.

Mayhew, Thomas. *A declaration about a vessel of William Weeks taken by Indians at one of the Elizabeth Isles*, Mass. Archives, State House, Boston, Mass.

Stowe, John. *Annals or a General Chronicle of England* . . . , London, 1631.

Strachey, William. *The historie of travaile into Virginia Britannia*, ed., R. H. Major (Hakluyt Society, 1st ser., VI), 1849.

Sturgess, H. A. C. *Register of Admissions to the Honourable Society of the Middle Temple*, 3 vols., London, 1949.

Winthrop, John. *Selections from an ancient Catalogue of objects of natural history formed in New England* . . . , Boston Athenaeum, Boston, 1727.

SECONDARY AUTHORITIES

Aknigg, G. P. V. *Shakespeare and the Earl of Southampton*, Harvard University Press, Cambridge, Mass., 1968.

Annonymous. *Historical Annals of Naushon*. L. H. Lowe Book Printer, Boston, 1901.

Annonymous. *Versus From the Island Book*, Riverside Press, Cambridge, 1865.

Annonymous. *Description of the Elizabeth Islands in Buzzards Bay*, New York, 1836.

Annonymous. *Penikese, A Reminisscence,* Frank H. Lattin, Albion, New York, 1895.

Banner, Earl. "Bartholomew Gosnold: Real Founder of this Country," *The Boston Globe,* 29 July, 1952.

Brown, Alexander C. "Reminiscences of the Last Voyage of the Bark Wanderer," *The American Neptune,* January, 1949.

Chamberlain, Barbara Blau. *These Fragile Outposts.* The Natural History Press, Garden City, New York, 1964.

Chute, M. *Shakespeare of London,* E. P. Dutton and Co., New York, 1964.

Coker, Robert E. "Fauna of Penikese Island," *Biological Bulletin,* Vol. 50, 1926.

Diamond, Sigmund. "Norembega: New England Xanadu," *The American Neptune,* April, 1951.

Emerson, Amelia Forbes. *Early History of Naushon Island,* Boston, 1935.

Emerson, Emilia Forbes, *Naushon Data,* Concord Press, West Concord, Mass., 1963.

Emerson, Ralph Waldo. *Letters and Social Aims,* Riverside Press, Cambridge, VIII, 1909.

Federal Writers Project of the Works Progress Administration. *Whaling Masters,* Old Dartmouth Historical Society, New Bedford, Mass., 1938.

Fogg, John M. "The Flora of the Elizabeth Islands," *Rhodora-Journal of New England Botanical Club,* Volume XXXII, 1930.

Forbes, Edith. *Historical Annals of Naushon,* Boston, 1901.

Forbes, John Murray. *Some Random Recollections of an Octogenarian,* Rockwell and Churchill Press, Boston, 1898.

Gookin, Warner F. and Barbour, Philip L. *Bartholomew Gosnold, Discoverer and Planter,* Archon Books, Hamden and London, 1963.

Gookin, Warner F. "The First Leaders at Jamestown," *Virginia Magazine of History and Biography,* April, 1950.

Gray, F. C. "Visit to Elizabeth Island," *American Review,* Vol. 5, 1817.

Hale, Edward Everett. *Discussions of the Drama: Prospero's Island,* Dramatic Museum of Columbia University, MCMIX, 1919.

Hall, Arthur Cleveland. "Cuttyhunk," *New England Magazine,* September, 1897.

Haskell, Louise T. *The Story of Cuttyhunk,* Bradbury-Waring Inc., New Bedford, Mass., 1953.

Hollick, Arthur. "A Reconnoissance of the Elizabeth Islands," *Annals of the New York Academy of Science,* Volume XIII, 14 January, 1901.

Holmes, Oliver Wendall. *The Autocrat of the Breakfast Table,* Riverside Press, Cambridge, 1858.

Howland, Alice Forbes. *Three Islands* . . . Boston, 1964.

Howland, Alice Forbes. The Story of Pasque and the Pasque Island Club," *Intelligencer,* Dukes County Historical Society, Edgartown, Mass., February, 1962.

Huden, John C. *Indian Place Names of New England,* Museum of the American Indian, Heye Foundation, New York, 1962.

Hughes, Sarah Forbes. *Letters and Recollections of John Murray Forbes,* The Riverside Press, Cambridge, 1899.

Lawrence, E. D. *Bacon Is Shakespeare,* John McBride Co., New York, 1910.

Lewis, I. F., ed. "The Flora of Penikese, Fifty Years After," *Rhodora — Journal of the New England Botanical Club,* October, 1924.

Maul, Edwin. "Notes on the Flora of Penikese Island," *Rhodora, Journal of the New England Botanical Club,* Vol. 63, 1961.

Ogburn, D. and Ogburn C. *Shake-Speare, The Man Behind the Name,* William Morrow and Co., New York, 1962.

Purrington, Philip. "Shakespeare, Gosnold and the Smoking Rocks," *The Bulletin,* Old Dartmouth Historical Society, New Bedford, Mass., Summer, 1959.

Rabb, Theodore K. *Enterprise and Empire,* Harvard University Press, Cambridge, Mass., 1967.

Ricketson, Daniel. *History of New Bedford,* New Bedford, 1858.

Rowse, A. L. *William Shakespeare,* Harper and Row, New York, 1963.

Rowse, A. L. *Shakespeare's Southampton,* Harper and Row, New York, 1965.

Shepard, Marshall and Wilson, Harold C. "Captain Gosnold and the New World," *Intelligencer,* Dukes County Historical Society, Edgartown, Mass., February, 1972.

Shepard, Marshall, *Our Enchanted Island,* Dukes County Historical Society, Edgartown, Mass., 1940.

Wall, Annie R. "Gosnold and his Colony at Cuttyhunk," Old Dartmouth Historical Society Sketches, New Bedford, Mass., 30 June, 1903.

Wallet, Francis. "James Bowdoin, Patriot Propogandist," *New England Quarterly,* September, 1950.

Watson, Elizabeth. "The Modern Settlement at Cuttyhunk," *Old Dartmouth Historical Society Sketches,* New Bedford, Mass., 30 June, 1903.

Wilson, Harold C. and Carr, William C. "Gosnold's Elizabeth's Isle: Cuttyhunk or Naushon?", *The American Neptune,* April, 1973.

Wilson, Harold C. "An Authority Questions Enough Credit Given Gosnold," *The Falmouth Enterprise,* 24 November, 1967.

Wilson, Harold C. "Gosnold: A Man and His Monument," *The Cape,* Orleans, Mass., Vol. 3, No. 1 and 2, 1968-69.

Wilson, Harold C. "Buzzards Bay alias Bay of Coves," *The Log,* Buzzards Bay Power Squadron, June, 1972.

Wilson, Harold C. "Student of Gosnold Analyzes John Brereton's Familiar Account," *The Falmouth Enterprise,* 18 May, 1971.

Wilson, Harold C. "Warner F. Gookin, Historical Detective," *Intelligencer,* Dukes County Historical Society, Edgartown, Mass., February, 1973.

Wilson, Harold C. and Carr, William C., *Bridges to Discovery,* unpublished manuscript.

Woodworth, Jay B. and Wigglesworth, Edward. *Geography and Geology of the Region Including Cape Cod, The Elizabeth Islands . . . ,* Memoirs of the Museum of Comparative Zoology at Harvard College, Cambridge, Mass., 1934.

POPULAR BOOKS AND ARTICLES

Brown, Alexander C. "Enchanted Voyage," *The American Neptune,* July, 1947.

Hill, Lee. *The Sharpie Sanderling,* Branden Press, Boston, 1971.

Kabbé, Gustov. "An Island of New England," *Century Magazine,* May, September, 1898.

Keyes, Langley Carleton. *Cape Cod Passage, A History of the Cape In Verse,* Reynolds-Dewalt Publishers, New Bedford, 1969.

Reynard, Elizabeth. *The Narrow Land,* Houghton Mifflin Co., 1968.

Shay, Edith and Shay, Frank, ed. *Sand In Their Shoes,* Houghton Mifflin Co., 1951.

Teller, Walter. *Cape Cod and the Offshore Islands,* Prentice Hall, New York, 1970.

Winston, Alexander. *No Man Knows My Grave,* Winston Publishers, New York, 1969.

"Literary Tempest Swirls Over Isles of Buzzards Bay," *Falmouth Enterprise,* 26 May, 1950.